Tara,

Trust Barry

Trust!.

Trust!

Selling in a Post-Trust World

Praise for *Selling in a Post-Trust World*

Larry's work is world-class and opens all of our hearts and minds to the most excellent profession in the world: serving others. Through sales, Larry teaches purpose with the opportunity to create and transfer value. The world needs more of Larry. *Selling in a Post-Trust World* should be required reading for every business in the world!

-**Don Barden,** senior economist and leadership expert, and author of *The Perfect Plan*

Larry Levine is one of my favorite human beings. Compassionate and driven, in appropriate amounts, Larry is a unique voice in the world of sales and beyond. There are many, many reasons to read his newest book, *Selling in a Post-Trust World*, but the most important one is the Trust Formula. Of course, to understand and apply that brilliance, you need to read the entire book. Being able to visualize a realistic and credible process to build real trust is a game-breaker when it comes to making sure you don't become one of the dreaded "empty suits."

-**Mike Garrison,** coach and author of *Can I Borrow Your Car?*

In September, 2018, Larry Levine published his game- and culture-changing best-seller, *Selling from the Heart.* This put Larry on a par with every world-class author that has ever linked selling to relationship development. Authenticity was the foundation of Larry's first book. Belief and conviction are at the core of *Selling in a Post-Trust World*. Inspiring stories, aspirational concepts, and practical applications dot every page, and the workbook is filled with tools and ideas to take your sales approach to a new level of success. *Selling in a Post-Trust World* provides insights about doing well by doing right and looking forward to greater results by looking inward to build unbreakable client trust through differentiated value.

-**Jack Hubbard**, chief experience officer, Jack Hubbard Consulting

The most perfect evolution of the original *Selling from the Heart*, *Selling in a Post-Trust World* is on point and relevant for the sales professionals navigating the storms and successes of the current climate. Every page has content that will resonate with those sales professionals who strive to build the best relationships and then want to continue to grow those relationships even further. Larry shares his extensive knowledge, which is cemented in his experience. This is what makes it so real and relatable.

-**Simon Hares**, managing director, Serial Trainer 7

There is a core message in *Selling in a Post-Trust World*: soft skills matter most. This is a must-read for managers, leaders, and salespeople at all levels. Emotional intelligence and soft skills like trust, authenticity, and relationships are the keys to success. Taking action on the advice in *Selling in a Post-Trust World* will set you on the path to success.

-**Lahat Tzvi**, founder and CEO, Tfisot

The subtitle of Larry Levine's newest book says it all: "Discover the soft skills that yield hard dollars." Larry dives deep into both the skillset and the mindset of the phenomenal sales pros who create meaningful value. Packed full of insights and inspiration, *Selling in a Post-Trust World* takes a sledgehammer to the wash/rinse/repeat philosophy that has overrun and overwhelmed the market. Buyers want something more, something authentic, and *Selling in a Post-Trust World* delivers exactly what they want from professional sellers. No more empty suits!

-**Tim Ohai**, growth architect and coach

When you read a sales book, you expect to be a better seller. Larry transcends the category by teaching sellers how to be better people. To win in a post-trust world, you don't need more sales tactics; you need to be a better you.

-**Nigel Green,** author of *Revenue Harvest* and an authority on building best-in-class sales teams

I am a big proponent of working on the right end of the problem. And *Selling in a Post-Trust World* does just that by specifically addressing how and why lack of authenticity leads to lack of trust. This, in turn, leads to missed revenue goals and, I might add, happiness goals. It's time to join the "no more empty suits" movement!

-Colleen Stanley, author of
Emotional Intelligence for Sales Leadership

Larry does a fantastic job providing the framework for using the trust formula to stand out in any industry. Nowadays, many professions are looking for shortcuts, simple processes, and sales hacks that bypass trust. Competent high-performing professionals understand that trust is the most critical ingredient in the sales process. Why? Because without trust, it will be impossible to sell anything to anyone. Omitting trust in the sales process is the fastest way to burn bridges and send your ideal clients and customers to your competitor. Today's consumers require more from sales professionals, and you can give them exactly what they are looking for when it comes to making confident buying decisions. Using Larry's trust formula will help you to authentically connect and build genuine relationships that lead to long-term success. Only some people are prepared or ready to do the deep inner work and sell with high trust, but those who boldly step into the trust arena will become top salespeople and business professionals.

-Liz Wendling, sales coach and author of
The Heart of Authentic Selling

You are the secret ingredient of your sales success. In *Selling from the Heart*, Larry gave you permission to love your customers. In *Selling in a Post-Trust World*, Larry gives you the formula for how to turn that emotion into long-term success. This is not the squishy subject it was once considered to be. It's the truth about what it takes to connect with other people and succeed at the highest levels.

-Jeff Bajorek, consultant, author, and host of the
Rethink the Way You Sell Podcast

Larry Levine has his hand firmly at the pulse of this growing *Selling from the Heart* movement he kickstarted, and *Selling in a Post-Trust World* is the perfect continuation for the world we are in. The way he navigates so effectively from real stories to experiences and references that hit close to home feels so effortless because it's clearly from the heart. Larry loves sales and shows it in how he teaches his audience to show up to serve, embrace a giving mindset, and build long-lasting, genuine relationships in sales. So many elements of selling have changed—from technology to perception of sellers—but Larry delivers relatable, practical, and inspirational advice that empowers us all to be more authentic.

-**Carson V. Heady,** author of *Salesman on Fire*
and Microsoft healthcare sales director

As a nerd for the history of the selling profession, modern-day writing has lost some of its luster. One hundred years ago, writing was an art, where every sentence consumed you, and you couldn't wait for the next. When I read *Selling in a Post-Trust World*, Larry brought me back to that time. He's written a masterpiece that lives its mantra of trust, where the writing is warm, draws you in, full of nostalgia, actionable, and, most of all, from the heart.

-**Todd Caponi,** author of *The Transparency Sale* and
The Transparent Sales Leader

Larry Levine's new book, *Selling in a Post-Trust World,* stresses personal growth and development as keys to success in business and sales. He emphasizes building relationships and creating meaningful value on the Trust Formula, by accessing positive traits such as curiosity and a servant's heart to establish human engagement and business stature. It is a timely and helpful read for those seeking success in these areas.

-**Bernadette McClelland,** author of *SHIFT and DISRUPT: Stop
Selling Widgets. Start Selling Wisdom.*

Through the generations, trust in business has been eradicated, but healthy relationships cannot exist without it. *Selling in a Post-Trust World* presents the recipe for relationships to flourish founded in deep trust that builds client loyalty.

-Lee B. Salz, sales management strategist and bestselling author
of *Sales Differentiation and Sell Different!*

Human connection is the number one contributor to happiness and success in all areas of our lives. *Selling in a Post-Trust World* inspires readers to be genuine, to truly care, and to connect to the meaning in their work. The soft skills that Larry teaches will transform people's personal lives and catapult them to more success and lasting relationships. We have never felt more disconnected in our ever-connected world, and *Selling in a Post-Trust World* gives people a proven framework to elevate their well-being and find the true joy in selling!

-Tia Graham, founder of Arrive at Happy and
best-selling author of *Be a Happy Leader*

In his latest book, *Selling in a Post-Trust World*, Larry Levine picks up where he left off in *Selling from the Heart* and gives us valuable tools like The Trust Formula, as well as guidelines for developing stronger, more authentic relationships. I have always struggled to develop strong relationships, so you shouldn't be surprised that I loved this self-help book for salespeople, and I'm sure you'll love it, too.

-Dave Kurlan, founder of Objective Management Group and CEO
at Kurlan & Associates

Business is not an impersonal email, or a nine-word text message, or ten-second voicemail. Business is about relationships and the people at either end of the relationship. As simple as this sounds, it's anything but simple when we're faced with the demands of business and life. Larry Levine is the calm voice you hear in the back of your head, the one that is nudging you to just be you and to take a few moments to be authentic with the person you're speaking to. Do yourself a favor as you read *Selling in a Post-Trust World*: don't read it fast; instead, read a page or two and stop to reflect on what you just read. *Selling in a Post-Trust World* is your compass; it's your North Star to becoming the authentic people-focused person you've always wanted to be.

-Mark Hunter, "The Sales Hunter"

Larry's two excellent books, *Selling from the Heart* and *Selling in a Post-Trust World*, in my estimation, should be the first two books any budding salesperson reads. They are, simply put, about positioning salespeople for success. Sadly, most salespeople typically start down the wrong path, becoming self-centered product pushers who have been programmed to SELL, SELL, SELL, when they should be serving their customers. This is not some "touchy-feely" concept; rather, professional consultative salespeople learn to think and act like business advisors who are focused on identifying and serving the needs of businesses. In *Selling in a Post-Trust World*, Larry's instructions about selling value, building business acumen, and developing trust are the bedrock for a successful sales career. My advice? Before you start training your salespeople on product knowledge, make these two books the first step in your training process!

-Kelly Riggs, founder, Business LockerRoom, Inc.

Selling in a Post-Trust World is a game-changer because it brings a breath of fresh air with its emphasis on authenticity, humanity, and empathy to both human and sales interactions! I've come across a lot of books on selling techniques in my twenty-plus year sales career, but it stands out because of its authentically genuine and heartfelt approach. *Selling in a Post-Trust World* not only shares invaluable insights, but also encourages readers to tap into their true selves and the value of connecting. One of my favorite statements in the book is, "When you change yourself, you start to view your sales life in a different manner. It is all about changing yourself to become a better individual; in turn, this will make the business world a better place." Larry has brilliantly used *Selling in a Post-Trust World* to remind us that behind every sale is a real person with real needs, and by connecting on a human level, we can build long-lasting, meaningful relationships with our customers.

    -Roderick Jefferson, enablement executive, keynote speaker, and best-selling author

SELLING IN A POST-TRUST WORLD

Discover the Soft Skills
that Yield Hard Dollars

LARRY LEVINE

Author of

SELLING from the **HEART**

NEW YORK

LONDON • NASHVILLE • MELBOURNE • VANCOUVER

SELLING IN A POST-TRUST WORLD

Discover the Soft Skills That Yield Hard Dollars

Published in New York, New York, by Morgan James Publishing. Morgan James is a trademark of Morgan James, LLC. www.MorganJamesPublishing.com

Scripture taken from the NEW KING JAMES VERSION®. Copyright© 1982 by Thomas Nelson, Inc. Used by permission. All rights reserved.

Scripture marked NASB are taken from the NEW AMERICAN STANDARD BIBLE®, copyright© 1960, 1962, 1963, 1968, 1971, 1972, 1973, 1975, 1977, 1995 by The Lockman Foundation. Used by permission.

Proudly distributed by Publishers Group West®

Connect with Larry Levine . . .

www.SellingFromTheHeart.net

www.linkedin.com/in/larrylevine1992/

E-Mail: LLevine@SellingFromTheHeart.net

ISBN 9781636983431 paperback
ISBN 9781636983448 ebook
Library of Congress Control Number: 2023947060

Cover Design by:
Jeremy B Clark
jeremybclark.com

Interior Design by:
Chris Treccani
www.3dogcreative.net

Morgan James PUBLISHING Builds with... **Habitat for Humanity** Peninsula and Greater Williamsburg

Morgan James is a proud partner of Habitat for Humanity Peninsula and Greater Williamsburg. Partners in building since 2006.

Get involved today! Visit: www.morgan-james-publishing.com/giving-back

Dedication

To my loving, supportive, caring, and beautiful wife, Robin . . . our relationship continues to strengthen and flourish as we've ridden the entrepreneurial rollercoaster together. You've always believed in me even when I struggle to believe in myself. Our love continues to grow throughout all of these years because we've always been real with each other. You make me stronger. You've been my biggest fan as I continue to travel down the road less taken.

To the Selling from the Heart *community, I love you. All of this doesn't happen without your support. Relationships are the cornerstone of human connection. Make sure your relationships are real, relatable, and relevant. Heart prevails in a world full of empty suits.*

Table of Contents

Acknowledgments

One very powerful realization is that everything happens for a reason. I believe these moments prepare us for what's to come in life. It helps us to get ready for a bigger and brighter future.

You can't have the pleasure of success without suffering through the pain of defeat. That moment for me was the spring of 2015. Being forced to transition careers in my 50s taught me a lot about myself and what I was capable of creating.

As my dear friend Dave Sanderson often says, "Moments matter." I believe it's what we do with these moments that matter the most.

For me, the pivotal moment was creating the *Selling from the Heart* podcast in April of 2017 with my dear friend Darrell Amy. I had no idea who would listen or even pay attention to us.

I am proud to say the podcast helped to launch my first book, *Selling from the Heart*. When the book was released, I had no idea if 5, 50, 500, or 5,000 books would sell. Heck, I was clueless as to what would happen next. I had no idea that it would turn into a business or create a movement around authenticity inside the sales profession.

In reality, I turned all of what I learned from my close inner circle and applied radical amounts of action to turn *Selling from the Heart* into what it is today. It is what I learned from my experiences that gave all of this reason.

To Mark Hunter and Mike Weinberg: you guys have been right there by my side this entire journey. Your mentorship, guidance, encouragement, advice, and belief in me have kept me staying in my lane.

To Bernadette McClelland: you helped me bring *Selling from the Heart* to life with your wonderful foreword. Your friendship, encouragement, and that shoulder to lean on has helped me see through the light.

To Dave Sanderson: when we connected in September of 2020, I had no idea the impact you would have on me professionally and personally. Your coaching and mentoring provided me with certainty during uncertain times. You and Terri will always be a part of my life.

To Don Barden: there are certain people you meet in life that just give it to you straight. Well, my man, you're one of them. The amount of advice and guidance you have provided me is priceless.

To Hugh Hornsby: I believe you meet people at the right time and for the right reasons. From day one, our conversations got deep fast. I value our friendship. Every time we speak, I know it is going to be heartfelt and sincere.

To Jackie Joy: there is no way that our journey together could have been scripted any better. I remember when we first connected, you mentioned, "You wrote this book for me." Never in a million years could I have predicted that you would play such an integral part in *Selling from the Heart*.

To Darrell Amy: there are not enough words, phrases, and pages inside this book that could express my heartfelt gratitude. I remember the conversation we had back in 2015. You saw something in me that I didn't see in myself. Our journey together has been an epic rollercoaster. You have brought out things in me that I never thought were possible. More importantly, we've done this together.

To Tim Ohai: this friendship I owe a huge thank you to Mike Weinberg. He became the bridge to one of the most special friendships I have. What has made it this way is we have poured into each other from day one. We have shared so many deep conversations, both personally and professionally. You truly are a gift.

To Bill McCormick: a huge thank you. You came into my life at the right time in my journey. I am super-grateful to you for introducing me to the message of Craig Groeschel.

To serve is the ultimate form of giving back. A special shout-out to my Thousand Oaks Kiwanis family…the friendships formed have been life-changing for me. We all unite under the common theme of giving back. As the illustrious Bob Engler always says, "Many hands make light work."

The journey in bringing both *Selling from the Heart* and *Selling in a Post-Trust World* to the forefront would have been insurmountable without Kim Thompson-Pinder and her team at RTI Publishing. You will always have a special place in my heart. You've witnessed *Selling from the Heart* grow up.

To David Hancock and his team at Morgan James Publishing: thank you. Your belief in me has allowed me to bring this *Selling from the Heart* movement to a wider audience.

To the most important person in my life, Robin, my beautiful wife: you've been my rock, my shoulder to lean on, and my biggest fan. I would not be here today if it wasn't for your support, encouragement, and belief in me. I love you.

In a world that lacks so much trust, my hope for all of you is that the message inside *Selling in a Post-Trust World* inspires you to take action, rising above all others, as you catapult your way to even greater success.

Foreword

The book you are now holding, or streaming through your Air-Pods, is much more than a formula for achieving breakthrough success in sales; it is a manual for building meaningful, mutually beneficial, joy-giving, and lifelong relationships!

It is rare when a literary work is perfectly timed and precisely crafted to address a situation that is urgent *and* critically important. Larry Levine's *Selling in a Post-Trust World* is that work.

This book is titled perfectly. We are indeed living (and attempting to sell) in a post-trust world. Everywhere you turn, there is deep skepticism—and unfortunately, it's deserved. Truly, *this* is the issue of the day. We are inundated with artificial intelligence, deep fakes, spam, and bots.

On top of all the technology fostering buyers' mistrust of sellers, add to this the lack of mentoring and coaching that has led to a generation of salespeople deploying awful, trust-busting processes. These include the all-too-common LinkedIn "invite then pitch," mass impersonal outreach, the bait and switch, *spray and pray*, and demo before discovery, all of which causes them to come across as the self-absorbed, transactional, uncaring, and unprofessional salespeople that Larry unapologetically labels as *empty suits.*

To make matters worse, there is no shortage of charlatans in the "sales improvement" business, peddling their supposedly foolproof cures for all that ails your sales. These hucksters boldly and shamelessly proclaim that their tools, tricks, approaches, and schemes are your short-cut to sales success. Cadences, automation, slick tools, quick hacks—all of these come across as selfish and inauthentic, which is the antithesis of what Larry has been preaching since the inception of his *Selling from the Heart* movement.

The simple reason my sales friends that Larry Levine's message of authenticity, congruence, credibility, and generosity is so popular is because it works! I have been following Larry for a decade. I'm honored to call him a friend. With Larry, what you see and what you hear is what you get. It's who he is: the most giving and authentic person in our profession. He's the walking, talking example of congruence and integrity. He lives what he preaches, and he penned this book because he desperately wants to help you thrive with selling in this post-trust world.

We all know and love to repeat this popular idiom: *people buy from people they like and trust.* Larry's *Trust Formula*, which he unveils in the introduction and powerfully unpacks with examples throughout the book, breathes life into this expression and shows us exactly how to become more likable and trustworthy throughout every stage of the sales cycle.

I love this book because I love sales. I bleed sales. I am pro-sales and, like Larry, proud to have a voice supporting the sales community. I screamed "yes" and "amen" while reading my advance copy more times than I could count because the approaches and techniques you are about to read (or hear) will help you, as this book's subtitle promises, discover the soft skills that yield hard dollars. These are the very skills that make top salespeople top salespeople!

Embrace the wisdom from the pages that follow, and you are guaranteed to exhibit increasingly more of Larry's 3 Rs (real, relatable, relevant) that radically increase sales effectiveness.

Here's to your breakthrough success with selling in this post-trust world.

-Mike Weinberg
Author of *New Sales. Simplified.*, *Sales Truth*,
and *The First-Time Manager: Sales*

Testimonial

Scott MacGregor,
Founder and CEO of SomethingNew LLC,
and Founder of The Outlier Project

A lot has changed since Larry's first book *Selling from the Heart* came out in 2018. Larry's Dodgers won a World Series and his Rams won a Super Bowl. My Yankees and Minnesota Vikings… well, not so lucky! What hasn't changed is my endearing friendship with Larry. The time-tested principles that Larry wrote about in *Selling from the Heart* haven't changed and they never will. This is what makes his writing so relevant. He doesn't write about fads; he writes about and teaches values that will make you a better person, both personally and professionally. That's why I was so excited when Larry gave me the honor of adding a few words to his second book, which is exceptional.

Authentic relationships are sometimes hard to come by. Why is that? Well, one reason is that they take work. They don't just happen, and they certainly don't grow over time without effort. Another factor is that they take a mutual commitment to helping other people even when there seems to be nothing in it for you. When you do these things, you gain credibility and trust, which are foundational elements of building true authentic relationships.

Larry and I started our entrepreneurial journey around the same time. We've seen the good, the bad, and the ugly of what it takes to build something from scratch. One of the things that is vital in getting you through challenging times are these authentic relationships. They become the sounding board, the proverbial shoulder to cry on, the mentor, the accountability partner, and the friend who is like an insurance policy because they are always there. All of these things are critical for our success, but again, they don't simply happen.

We began talking on a regular basis in 2015 and through those conversations, I could see Larry's heart. By understanding his unwavering commitment to do the right thing and to grow as a person, I developed a deep trust long before we ever met in person. From there, it became very natural to show up for each other. We've both written in each other's books, been involved in each other's communities, been active promoters of each other, and liberally and generously made valuable strategic introductions. None of those things would have happened if there wasn't a high level of trust.

When my first book *Standing O!* came out, Larry and his incredible wife Robin hopped on a plane and flew from LA to NYC to support me and celebrate at the launch party. We still to this day talk about our wives dancing on The Refinery Hotel Rooftop the day after, and talking about our dreams of what we both wanted to accomplish next.

Sharing your dreams is like blowing on a fire: it makes it come alive and makes it bigger. However, sharing dreams isn't done with just anyone. Again, you need trust and support. We both have had ideas that the other saw opportunities to make better or even to avoid altogether. When you have mutual respect, that feedback can save you a ton of time, aggravation, and money. It can also take a good idea and make it a great one. Sometimes, that feedback can be the difference between creating a zero or a hero idea. Don't we all want that honest, caring, thoughtful, and smart feedback? This only comes from the investments and deposits we make in other people, and from them reciprocating with the same.

Tactically, this book is about how to avoid transactional selling or, as Larry would say, "being an empty suit", and how to be truly consultative. After all, who doesn't want to be the trusted advisor?

Ultimately, though, this book is about authentic relationships, and this is why it should be required reading for everyone. We enhance our own lives and the lives of many others when we show up as our authentic self and build meaningful, long-lasting relationships.

Larry is a master at guiding you down that path with the life lessons he has learned and from being an entertaining storyteller. He's an exceptional teacher and because he walks the talk, his credibility on this topic is never in doubt. This might be Larry's second book, but I hope it's not his last because he writes with such clarity and wisdom that the world needs more.

Hopefully, by the time book number three comes out, I'll be celebrating some championship trophies. However, if I am or not, I know that Larry will be there with a story or a joke because that's what friends do.

Preamble

by Dave Sanderson,
Speaker, Author, and Philanthropist

What is an authentic relationship? They begin when we put down our veil and show our true self to another person. You must become vulnerable in what you communicate and how you act. It's a true sign of respect when you show your true self to another human being.

One word I use consistently is "congruent." I first learned this word and concept when I was assistant head of security for noted speaker and philanthropist Tony Robbins. I was standing on stage left, having Tony's back, and he started to dissect the 1996 U.S. election. There were many reasons why some people won and why some lost, Tony explained, but the results usually came down to who was most congruent. The person who was consistent with what they said and did is what most people were looking for in their leaders. In a relationship, it means being true to yourself, understanding who you are, and knowing what is most important to you. Congruency allows you to be in total rapport with yourself first and then with your relationships.

For many years, I was incongruent. I was not honest with myself. I often felt that I had to "keep up with the Joneses", and it cost me financially, emotionally, and with relationships. Fortunately, my mentor Bill was the most congruent person I had ever met (other than my father). He walked his talk and taught me the importance of being consistent with what I said and did. Bill not only showed me what it meant to be congruent, but told me that in business, it was rare when you interacted or worked with someone who is congruent, and I would stand out if I was one of the few who walked their talk. That one lesson helped me not only grow in my business relationships, but also with my wife, children, and friends.

The challenge with not being congruent emanates with a lack of trust we end up generating with the people in our lives. It is difficult to trust someone if they behave in a way that is contrary to what they think or believe.

When I first met Larry Levine and his movement, *Selling from the Heart*, the first thing that stood out was what you see with Larry is what you get. Larry and I have similar backgrounds. We both were in copier sales. We both have the instinct to help others grow, and we both are focused on authentic relationships with people that are congruent.

Selling from the Heart is based on being congruent with the relationships we have, both professionally and personally. It focuses on a few key attributes that attract sales associates and entrepreneurs from across the world.

As I have worked with Larry and watched what attracts people to him and his movement, I've identified these key attributes.

First, Larry pays attention to what his relationships are feeling and thinking. He takes the time to understand where his relationships are in their life so he can serve them where they are at and help them get to where they want to go.

Second, Larry doesn't hide behind any facades. He is out in front and will gladly tell and show his clients and relationships about his movement. *Selling from the Heart* is out front and doesn't have anything to hide.

One thing I learned years ago was when I was wrong, own it. Larry is an example of that. None of us are perfect. Many people today will not own up to their mistake. They will evade, deny, or blame someone else. A significant part of having an authentic relationship is to "own up" when we make a mistake and work to make it good. I have made many mistakes in my life and there were times when I wouldn't own up to them. However, I learned from my mentors that people will respect you and will want to have an authentic relationship with you if you do so. Larry is consistent with this. When something goes sideways, he goes overboard to make it right, which is a key factor to why Larry has so many authentic relationships.

One of Larry's strengths is that if he doesn't have an answer to something, he admits it. I'm sure there have been times in Larry's life that he blurted out an answer before thinking through it (we all have done that). Still, with time comes wisdom, and I feel one of the main reasons Larry has so many authentic relationships is because he recognizes he may not be the right person to give an answer, and people respond to someone who has enough self-confidence to admit that.

Larry has been a role model for me and has helped me grow in my personal life and in my entrepreneurship. As I have coached Larry on what my mentors have taught me about leading yourself first, a part of that is being congruent with the relationships you have. Relationships are not one way; it's a two-way street. Larry has taught me that trust, being yourself, and standing behind your word are essential to being a top producer and are needed more today than ever before.

When you read *Selling in a Post-Trust World: Discover the Soft Skills That Yield Hard Dollars*, you will not only learn key factors to help you in your career, but you'll come to understand that with authentic relationships, you can create your own flight plan for your future.

Dave Sanderson
Speaker, Author, and Philanthropist

Preface

*Become the person who would attract
the results you seek.*
Jim Cathcart

The day after *Selling from the Heart* was launched, I received a phone call from two associates and dear friends of mine: Mark Hunter and Mike Weinberg. They asked, "Have you seen what your book's doing on Amazon? You're out-pacing very well-known authors. What's the secret here?" Honestly, I had not been paying much attention.

Quite frankly, I did not have a massive marketing budget or a publicist. I simply asked people for help. I humbled myself, and the community I built rose to the occasion, supported my efforts, and bought the book. Ultimately, the book's recipe for success was due to educating, engaging, and exciting people into having conversations. Add the secret ingredient of doing it from the heart, and the results speak for themselves.

Mark Hunter (author of *A Mind for Sales* and *High-Profit Prospecting*) is a key mentor and influencer in my life. So, being recognized by him was a pivotal moment for me after my book came out.

Early on, Mark gave me some monumental advice: "Larry, bring your book to life! Bring the message from each chapter of your book to life. Learn how to turn your book into a business. Give it 18 months and see what it becomes."

What he meant was for me to leverage each chapter in order to coach sales leaders and their teams. He thought I should allow the book to become bigger than I was, and then watch what happened.

Almost 18 months later, he and I were having coffee at a sales conference in Orlando, Florida, and he teased me by asking when my book had come out. Naturally, his projections had proved true, and I owe a great deal to Mark for both his inspiration and encouragement to bring the book to life.

Selling from the Heart has afforded me to travel the world, working closely with global corporations, sharing the book's core message, inspiring people, and building a movement around it. With discipline and consistency, I got the message out. It began to resonate, especially during the COVID-19 pandemic, as leadership started re-evaluating what people—and genuine relationships—meant to them.

I decided it was time to double down on my efforts to get the message out. I created virtual team sales meetings, deep-dive team-reads for the book, and virtual workshops along with coaching. The result was a groundswell and movement of bringing sincerity, substance, and heart to the forefront of relationships.

Someone I admire and respect is Davin Salvagno who runs an organization called PurposePoint. I have had the opportunity to speak at his Purpose Summit, and he has been on the *Selling from the Heart* podcast. In one of our conversations, he said, "Larry, you're creating a movement of authenticity in the sales profession. You're willing to talk about things that a lot of people think about, but they're uncomfortable talking about."

To this day, I am still taken aback by all the success and impact that the book has had. I still pinch myself every day. Honestly, I do—I have the bruises to prove it.

Words matter and so does your message. Still, it is how we *use* the words to get the message across. *Selling from the Heart* is not just a book that you read, it is a work that you internalize, and it becomes your sales lifestyle.

Mending Broken Hearts

I had not considered the impact that the self-reflection journal would have on my readers until years later. People who have committed to do the work have seen incredible transformation in how they view themselves, how they view their clients, and how they go about their business.

I stand before you right now and tell you: it helped me, too. I learned a tremendous amount about myself. I was able to dig in deep to identify issues that I have had in the past, work through them, and pour my newfound insight into the book to benefit others.

A signature moment on the *Selling from the Heart* podcast is when we ask each guest, "What does it mean to you to sell from the heart?" One guest floored me when they said, "It's hard to sell from the heart if your heart is broken." I could not have predicted the book's role and impact within the sales community to help mend broken hearts. All of this still blows my mind. I am a firm believer that things happen for a reason.

It is hard to emotionally connect to your clients, if your heart is broken. The hurt and pain hidden within keeps you from building true relationships because you are always protecting yourself from further pain, rejection, and suffering.

Unfortunately, there are not enough people in sales working on— or from—their heart, working on the inner part of who they really are. Authenticity is a lifestyle, not a light switch. It can be tough, but the field of sales is tough; it is a full-contact sport.

I can look back on all my years in sales and there was not one conference, sales training, or workshop that I ever attended where they said, "Hey, guess what, over the next few days we're going to work on the inner part of who we are. We're going to help you become the best version of you by working not only on skillset, but heart-set and mindset."

No More Empty Suits!

I have learned that you write your next book when your audience and the community start asking for one. For me, that's been happening for quite some time. The only way of continuing from *Selling from the Heart* is to pick up on where the final chapter left off: Chapter 10: "No More Empty Suits!"

The entire concept behind "an empty suit" is not meant to disrespect or cast a dark shadow over the sales community; it's to get leadership and salespeople thinking differently. It's about helping them see that if they are not educating and engaging with their clients; if they are not helping them do better business; if they are not helping them bring the future to the present; if they do not have their best interest at heart, and most importantly, if they are not building deep meaningful relationships based upon trust, then they are going to be viewed as being an empty suit. Such a suit looks good on the outside, but on the inside, it's nothing of importance.

I am writing this book to peel back the layers and assist you in uncovering what it means to build rock-solid, sincere, veracious, and trusted relationships. You must be willing to identify the gaps you have and become relational bridge builders.

Unfortunately, salespeople have been viewed through a negative set of lenses. They've been described as sleazy, slime-balls . . . you name it. The purpose behind this book is to drive home a critical point: if you want to remove the empty suit label, you must get real with yourself and your clients. There are no ifs, ands, or buts! The question then becomes: Are you willing to go on that journey?

It is time for leadership and those in sales to measure up, rise up, and bring professionalism back into the greatest profession there is: sales.

Digest every page of this book, commit to doing the work, and most of all, take massive action. Buckle up; our journey together is going to be an emotional roller coaster, but a positive one that will lead you to sales nirvana.

Introduction: Where Is the Trust?

When you take time to replenish your spirit,
it allows you to serve from the overflow.
You cannot serve from an empty vessel.
Eleanor Brown

According to the *Urban Dictionary*, an empty suit is someone puffed up with their own importance, but who has little effect on the lives of others. An empty suit conjures up the image of a business suit without a person in it who truly knows what he or she is doing.

There's absolutely nothing wrong with dressing the part. The problem lies when it is all style and no substance. Expensive name brand suits are no substitute for business acumen or business substance.

An empty suit lacks the sparkle in the eye, that, *"Je ne sais quoi."* They struggle to engage people in talking about their true passions. It is about being humble, curious, and giving a rip—three things an empty suit struggles to comprehend.

Often, when their clients and future clients share their heartfelt problems, the response from empty suits is a solid stream of buzzwords, canned pitches, and sales jargon. Instantaneously, it becomes painfully obvious that they have no empathy, no clue of their concerns, or how they may help them.

This, my sales friends, is an empty suit.

According to *Creating and Delivering Your Value Proposition* by David Pinder, "The term value proposition is used ubiquitously in business today and its original meaning has been dissipated into vague sales and marketing notions that are a million miles from its intended meaning and use."

Sales professionals know the "why" behind their value proposition. They deliver their value statement in a way that captures the hearts and minds of their clients. How well do your clients know and understand the value you bring? When was the last time you asked them?

It boils down to serving and delivering measurable amounts of value. You must live, walk, talk, and broadcast it for everyone to hear. Know thy value, and know thy self.

In today's crazy, busy world, we have an abundance of technology platforms to help salespeople do their job better and more efficiently. What concerns me is that we have forgotten the heart is at the center of sales.

I am bothered that many in our profession continually hide behind technology while dehumanizing sales. A heartfelt professional leverages technology to humanize their network and client relationships.

A sales professional remains one step ahead of their clients. This requires them staying current on trends while keeping their skills sharpened. Consistent education provides sales professionals with the readiness to embrace new ways of doing things, especially if the old ways are no longer cutting it.

Today's buyers expect, and to be candid, demand that salespeople understand their business, guiding them to solutions that target their specific challenges, initiatives, goals, and business dreams. They are well prepared and come to the business table with particular expectations. Thus, you need to be equally, if not more, prepared than they are.

The lack of preparation shows, as empty suits fail to capitalize on these conversations:

> ➢ The challenges the buyer faces.
> ➢ The barriers these challenges present to them.
> ➢ How to quantify the cost of a status quo mindset.
> ➢ What can you learn from them?

They struggle to ask deep, meaningful business questions and intentionally listen. Their lack of business substance, business acumen, and poor business conversational skills leads to emptiness syndrome. Empty suits struggle with competent conversations.

Selling from the Heart **Continues**

The foundation for this book was born in Chapter 10 of *Selling from the Heart*, "No More Empty Suits."

At the end of *Selling from the Heart*, I left you with my favorite poem by Robert Frost, "The Road Not Taken." To set this up, let's look at the ending of the poem:

> *I shall be telling this with a sigh*
> *Somewhere ages and ages hence:*
> *Two roads diverged in a wood, and I—*
> *I took the one less traveled by,*
> *And that has made all the difference.*

In the poem, there is someone standing in a yellow wood with two distinct paths before them. They look and think about both paths, and finally choose to take the one less traveled. Thus, they prefer experiencing something new without worrying about the consequences.

What sales road are you taking?

> *Entrepreneurs pay the price of a road less traveled,*
> *while everyone else takes the freeway and perpetually*
> *misses their own exit.*
> **Ryan Lilly**

Are you creating your own flight plan, or are you traveling down the same road as all the other salespeople just because it is safe? Genuine sales professionals forge their own path. It first starts at the intersection of self-alignment and knowing who you are. It is difficult to become the best version of yourself if you wrestle to identify with who you are and why you do what you do.

When you know your "why", you will know your way!

This struggle of misalignment to the inner self leads to sales chaos and the empty suit. When there's alignment, people sense it. They take

notice of it, and they welcome it. People understand when you're bringing the business goods. They sense when you are leaning into them, or
when you are pushing them to do something they may not want.

Sincerity in sales means truly listening, being genuine, honest, and
doing what is right. This lies at the heart of great selling. You must truly
care, understand your client's genuine needs, then deliver relevant solutions offering real value.

The Trust Formula

Unfortunately, we live in a post-trust sales world. Trust in sales is at
an all-time low. In fact, it's so low that one can step right over it without
even trying.

The widespread mistrust within the sales world both concerns and
saddens me. When it comes to salespeople, a stereotypical mindset runs
rampant within our society and in business.

Gallup is a global analytics and advice firm that helps leaders and
organizations solve their most pressing problems. In their survey ending
December 2020, salespeople and politicians were tied at 8 percent for the
lowest rating regarding trustworthiness, honesty, and ethics, while the
nursing profession topped out at 89 percent. What makes this percentage
so high? The answer is simple: nurses lead with empathy and heart. Can
the same be said for salespeople and their leadership?

Trust is the foundation of all deep and meaningful relationships. It
is what makes us feel safe being vulnerable to one another. Trust allows
relationships to endure through challenging times. Without trust, there is
no togetherness and very little long-term potential for a relationship to
flourish and deepen.

When it comes to trust, perception is in the eye of the beholder—
your clients. I believe perception feedback is necessary for bridging relational growth and trust with your clients. Regrettably, trusted relationships and promise bridges are crumbling as moments of betrayal are all
too fresh in their mind.

Shattered dreams and broken hearts have left many clients feeling
abandoned and neglected.

This is further reinforced with the Edelman DXI report, "Measuring Thought Leadership Report" November 2021, where they say, "Trust trumps reputation."

In this review, they go on to say that both trust and reputation are correlated with the intent to purchase, but that trust is in many ways the more powerful factor. Case in point: 61 percent of people globally say that a good reputation may get them to try a product. However, unless they come to trust the company behind the product, they will soon stop buying it regardless of its reputation.

Let's apply and relate this to salespeople. Unless your current and future clients come to trust you, they will soon stop buying from you regardless of your reputation.

We overcome this problem by walking, talking, living, and breathing trust. We must become congruent with our actions and bring our authentic self forward. As Russ Thoman states, "Trust vanishes the moment customers sense sellers are more interested in making the sale than in making sure customers feel a purchasing decision is best for them."

The challenge with trust is that you cannot fake, buy, or force it. Your clients cannot be coerced to believe you are trustworthy. You must be diligent with your actions to earn their confidence. Every interaction is an opportunity to deepen, build, and nurture trust.

- ➢ You must become genuinely interested in their business.
- ➢ You must truly connect with meaning.
- ➢ You must be honest and curious.
- ➢ You must actually care.

In a world full of empty suits, where relational gaps are monumental, one can bridge the trust and credibility gaps to sales success through the following formula:

Authentic Relationship (AR) plus Meaningful Value (MV), with the multipliers being Inspirational Experiences (IE) and Disciplined Habits (DH).

(AR + MV) x IE x DH = Trusted Relationships

This, in other words, is the **Trust Formula.**

The focal point of this book focuses on your relationship with yourself (not being an empty suit), while integrating the Trust Formula to create amazing relationships with your clients, potential clients, and your network. Add the 3 Rs (being real, relatable, and relevant), and watch what starts to happen to your sales growth.

Your Relationship with Yourself

In the beginning of this chapter, we dove into what an empty suit looks like. Throughout our time together, we will explore the relationship you have with yourself and how this affects how the world views you.

Are you staying true to yourself, or are you trying to be someone else? Are there things in your past that are holding you back from being your best self? Are you continually running your "emotional gas tank" on empty? Are you afraid that if your clients saw the real you, they would not want to work with you? Does imposter syndrome eat at your soul?

It does not have to be this way. I will share my journey with you, and how I dealt with these issues to become my true, authentic self, so you can, too.

Relationship Capital

It is crucial to double-down and invest in your relationships.

You must remain actively interested in your clients, not only when there is a sale to be made, but always! Your goal is to continually seek out areas to improve their business, actively listen, and intentionally learn how to support your clients.

You should lead with dignity, integrity, and the best version of yourself.

Relationship capital is without monetary value. It is intangible, but also indispensable. If you are failing to connect at deep meaningful levels with your clients, then how can you help them do better business?

Let's stop for a moment and consider what constitutes a relationship, not only to you but above all, to your clients. Investing in relationships is akin to traditional investing. If you never put any money into investing, there will not be any (plus interest) when you need it later on.

Therefore, if we fail to invest in our relationships, then we will never be able to collect on them either. We must constantly nurture, grow, and fertilize our relationships at higher rates than we ever have before. Simply put, relationships drive business.

Transactional conversations and only seeing customers as numbers is 100 percent replaceable. In a world where relationships matter, you must learn how to move your engagements from transactional to transformational.

I challenge and encourage you to branch out from the short-term, thirty-day, and quarterly sales thinking, and strive for long-term transformational relationships.

Short-term thinking stunts long-term sales sustainability. Dig in deep to continually educate, engage, and learn as much as you can about your clients. Consistently help them uncover areas to improve their business, even if you are not the one to get them there.

Buyers, executives, and your clients are smarter than you think. They expect more out of salespeople than ever before. If you care about your clients, you must invest in them. If not, they are going to view you as being nothing more than an empty suit.

Here's something to think about: "How are you connecting and relating to your clients and future clients?" To quote Pastor Chris Hodges of the Church of the Highlands, "In order to change our world, we need to connect before we correct."

As a society, the currency of how we relate to each other has changed, including sales. I believe the currency of sales is measured in specific outcomes: memories and experiences.

Professional sporting events and amusement parks do a tremendous job in creating and capturing these outcomes. Despite the ever-increasing price of admission, people continue to go, year after year, at record rates. There is zero price negotiation! Why? Because they have successfully mastered capturing memories and experiences, transcending monetary value.

You might be saying, "Well, wait a minute. I sell products, services, and solutions." Yes, but you are also selling outcomes. What memories and experiences are you creating for your clients?

Just for moment, I would like for you to reflect upon your own memories and experiences—the who, what, where, and why behind them. Now, think about this through the lens of your clients; does this take on a completely different meaning for you?

How does your relationship capital measure up?

Real, Relatable, and Relevant

Real

Your clients want to connect to, and do business with, a sales professional who sells from the heart, as opposed to a sales rep who is an empty suit.

In other words, they want to do business with somebody real, relatable, and relevant. Start living and breathing your real, unique, and fully authentic self.

Being real with your clients starts with being real with yourself. You must be willing to do the deep inner work around the heart, mind, and body. You must grab on to who you really are, bringing realness to the forefront. Become the most powerful version of yourself.

Be who you really are: your own unique piece of artwork—not a giclee or photographic-reproduced version of yourself. Stay true to who you are, and do not be swayed by what other people think. Allow your personality to shine like a diamond through every interaction; how you show up is going to be different than how somebody else shows up.

I would like for you to reflect upon the following:

> ➢ Are you fired up with enthusiasm and passion for what you do?
> ➢ Are you exciting your clients into wanting to know more?

Being excited and having passion is not a sales act; it is a lifestyle. It is woven into your personal DNA. Maintain a true passion for who you are, what you are selling, who you are becoming, and what you believe in.

A true sales professional is proactive. When you look at them, you notice high energy. They have magnetic personalities. They make things happen instead of sitting back and waiting for them to happen. They choose not to rest on their laurels. They have a positive attitude, are in control, and most of all, they believe in themselves.

When you call on your clients with energy and enthusiasm, it means you believe in yourself. Excitement is contagious. This isn't bravado; it's a sincere belief in yourself and that what you do cannot be faked. You must become a sales guide by bringing the business goods. You must facilitate and educate, instead of showing up and throwing up.

Relatable

Being relatable means being able to emotionally connect to your clients. Show them you understand how they feel and what they are going through. Empathize with them, and demonstrate your willingness to care for and help them. Pour yourself into your clients by connecting with them at deep, emotional levels. Then, watch what starts to happen next!

Unfortunately, at some point within your sales career, you may have been on the receiving end of this statement: "I'm sorry to inform you, but we decided to take our business elsewhere. Please don't take this personally; it is simply a business decision." I am here to tell you that business is personal and the more personal you make it, the greater the rewards.

Marcus Lemonis is a self-made millionaire, the host of the CNBC show *The Profit*, and the CEO of Camping World. He refuses to believe that business is not personal and has often been quoted saying, "This idea that business isn't personal is total BS. Business is personal."

He goes on to say,

> *I'm a big believer that in business, consumers will rally around a cause or a story or some personal connection that they have. People like to do business with people. It's OK that you amplify who you are; that's how I make a connection with you [as a consumer].*

The method of making business personal is simple: bring forward your authentic self and relate to people. Relate to the commonalities between you and your clients. Relate to their concerns, dreams, and aspirations. Offer your assistance, and invest in them. Look after them and their business.

I encourage all of you to:

> ➢ Be authentic. The foundation of trust is authenticity.
> ➢ Serve first. Be on the lookout to serve even if it does not pay off for you.

> ➢ Your clients are humans, not numbers. Listen to them and learn from them.
> ➢ Make it personal. Surprise and delight your clients.

The time is now. Wake up and stop taking advantage of your most precious asset: your clients.

Relevant

Relevancy is mission critical. It is defined as "the quality or state of being closely connected or appropriate." Once you have become woven into the fabric of a client's business, by listening with your heart, you become valued. If you are valued, you are relevant and vice versa.

Kavanah is a Hebrew word that implies sincerity, intention, and the direction of the heart. This means devotion, with complete focus, irrespective of surrounding chaos. I implore you to embrace this framework in your quest of not being another empty suit.

As we embark on this journey, ask yourself the following questions:

> ➢ Are you real with yourself? Are you real with your clients?
> ➢ Are you connecting to yourself? Are you connecting to your clients?
> ➢ Are you relevant? Are you relevant to your existing and future clients?
> ➢ Are you relevant in the marketplace?

As you do the work, you will be amazed at how your life and your sales career will change.

I invite you to join me on the road to self-discovery.

Head on over to www.sellinginaposttrustworld.com. There, you will find the Trust Formula Mini-Course, as well as free resources. It will help you take what you learn from our time together and apply it to your sales career.

Are you ready for the ride of your life? Turn to the next page.

Introduction Summary

1. An empty suit conjures up the image of a business suit without a person in it who truly knows what he or she is doing.
2. Genuine sales professionals forge their own path. It first starts at the intersection of self-alignment and knowing who you are. It is difficult to become the best version of yourself if you wrestle to identify with who you are and why you do what you do.
3. The Trust Formula. Authentic Relationship (AR) plus Meaningful Value (MV), with the multipliers being Inspirational Experiences (IE) and Disciplined Habits (DH).

(AR + MV) x IE x DH = Trusted Relationships

4. Are you afraid that if your clients and future clients saw the real you that they would not want to do business with you? Does imposter syndrome eat at your soul?
5. If we fail to invest in our relationships, then we will never be able to collect on them either. We must constantly nurture and grow our relationships at higher rates than we ever have before.
6. Your clients want to connect to, and do business with, a sales professional who sells from the heart, as opposed to a sales rep who is an empty suit.

INTRODUCTION—AUTHENTIC RELATIONSHIPS

The first part of the trust equation begins with Authentic Relationships (AR).

What does authenticity mean to you? Conversely, what does inauthenticity mean to you? How would you define both of these terms? When you can internalize, answer, and apply this to your client interactions, you then start the journey in transforming your client relationships.

The authentic relationships you build and nurture with your clients start with the authentic relationships you build with yourself.

I love this quote from David G. Benner from his book, *The Gift of Being Yourself . . . The Sacred Call to Self-Discovery*:

> *Our masks have become our reality, and we have become our lies. In short, we have lost authenticity and adopted an identity based on illusion. We have become a house of smoke and mirrors.*

To understand your authentic self, you must be willing to ditch the sales facades, charades, and masks. How do you feel about how you are portraying *yourself* to the business world? Are you truly being yourself? If you said yes, how would you know?

Do you feel that you can be yourself, no matter what sales situation you are in?

Masks may protect you; however, if you are not bringing the true version of yourself to the business table, then I am here to inform you that at some point you will get exposed. You may not believe me just yet, but I promise it is lurking just around the corner.

Mask wearing is a monumental drain on your mind. It is a hard act to repeatedly pretend to be, or feel like you need to be, someone else. Similarly, it is very draining to regularly act like you feel one way when you really feel another.

Sales masks are signs of weakness and stunt your sales growth. In the poem written by Charles C. Finn, "Please Hear What I Am Not Saying," the opening lines read:

> *Don't be fooled by me. Don't be fooled by the face I wear, for I wear a mask, a thousand masks, masks that I am afraid to take off and none of them is me.*

The longer you keep wearing the mask, the longer you will be fooling yourself.

Authenticity is a lifestyle and not a light switch. It is about congruency with who and what you are. How you act and how you carry yourself must be in alignment. Does your walk match your talk? Does your presentation to your clients match how you take care of them?

Building relationships with yourself and your clients is not a light switch you turn on and then off.

According to the *Free Dictionary*, a relationship is:

1. a connection, association, or involvement.
2. connection between people, kinship.
3. an emotional or other connection between people.

The happiness within your client relationships is mission critical to your sales growth. This happiness starts from within you. How happy are you with the relationship you have with yourself? Stop and think about it for a moment. When was the last time you sat down, had some quiet time, reflected, and thought about who you are and how you can best represent yourself to your clients?

Are you intentionally building the internal connection with yourself?

In *Selling from the Heart* (www.SellingFromTheHeart.net/book), I shared that if you want to have an ever-flowing sales funnel, you must build an ever-flowing relationship funnel. The relationship funnel becomes threatened when you are misaligned internally with the relationship you have with yourself.

This is a deep insight, but like the Bible says in John 8:32:

> "And you shall know the truth and the truth shall make you free."

I promise you at the conclusion of our journey together that this will all make sense.

When it comes to authentic relationships and the happiness with yourself and your clients, I would like for you to think about the following:

➢ What kind of a relationship is it?
➢ Has the relationship been mutually beneficial?
➢ Have both of your lives improved because of it?

Happy and healthy client relationships become the key to your sales growth. This all starts with the relationship you have with yourself, which we will explore in the next chapter.

Chapter 1:

Your Relationship
with Yourself

Peter left a potential client's office in total disbelief. His mind was racing, as he asked himself the question, "How could this have happened?" Moments earlier, that prospective client had informed him they would be doing business with someone else, and they did not require his company's service.

"I don't get it," Peter thought to himself, "I thought for sure this one was in the bag. I presented and shared with them everything they wanted to hear."

He decided before going back to work to face the music (aka, his sales manager) that he would grab a cup of coffee. He would take some time to reflect and put into words a way to share what had happened with his manager without getting thrown under the spotlight. (Does this scenario bring back memories?)

He chose a small corner table and sat down to commiserate. At the table next to him were two men nicely dressed, obviously celebrating a big business win. That made his misery even worse. Being in close proximity to them, he overheard their conversation. What Peter heard next would change his life forever.

"I can't believe we landed The Mutual Company. I thought for sure they were going with another company. When I asked them why they chose us, the COO mentioned the other company presented all the right things, but it was too much of a dog and pony show. They had worked with these types of salespeople before, and they never received what was promised. The only reason they kept them engaged was they had to present two quotes to the owners to show due diligence."

Peter shamelessly hung his head as he realized they had gotten the contract he had worked on. At that moment, the truth of the type of salesperson he was hit him squarely between the eyes. It was the wakeup call he needed and the beginning of Peter's journey to becoming a sales professional.

The Man in the Mirror

Our five senses (sight, sound, smell, taste, and touch) help us understand and perceive the world around us. Though not scientifically proven, I firmly believe that we all have a sixth sense. Mine is a keen awareness of BS, which has always helped me, but also played a toll on my mind, especially in my younger days.

When I look back on my sales career, spanning many decades, I was on more dysfunctional sales teams with more dysfunctional sales managers than I care to shake a stick at. It's an unfortunate practice and an unpleasant environment that still exists today.

My first year in sales was 1988. The #1 song that year was "Man in the Mirror" by Michael Jackson. It's a perfect song to consider as we start to bring the relationship with yourself to the forefront.

Admit it, as soon as I mentioned that song, you started singing it in your head. If not, go take a listen.

When you change yourself, you start to view your sales life in a different manner. It is all about changing yourself to become a better individual; in turn, this will make the business world a better place.

This is why focusing on the relationship with yourself is so critically important. You cannot control what happens around you, but you can control yourself and your actions. The mirror never lies, only the person looking into it.

My first year in sales was brutal. I was paid a draw against a monthly wage of $1,500.00 U.S. Keep in mind that this was 1988.

As a young, impressionable salesperson starting out in sales, I mirrored and mimicked what I perceived to be the top salespeople. I listened and focused in on what they were saying. I went on field ride-outs with them. I observed how they interacted with their customers and amongst themselves. I was committed to fitting in and being just like them. Can you sense where this is going? Does this sound all too familiar?

Months and months went by with no sales. I was hitting my new meeting weekly numbers. I was demonstrating products, and nothing was happening. I was emotionally drained, physically spent, and mentally worn down.

Then, at twenty-four years old, I had a mirror moment: was I being myself, or was I pretending to be someone I was not? I realized that I was mirroring the actions of others, and it was in direct conflict with who I was internally.

Remember that sixth sense of BS? Well I had bought into it and, in turn, I was letting the lies about me, my products, my company, and my commissions place a stranglehold on my consciousness. I let my sales environment dictate my thoughts and actions. This was holding me back emotionally and mentally, and the toll was immense.

It was not long after this realization that I made my first sale. By nature, I am very curious and love asking tons of questions, so I asked my first customer, "Why did you buy from me? And I don't want to hear you felt sorry for me."

What happened next started my journey from salesperson to sales professional. They said, "You were the only salesperson who didn't make it about their company, their product, or themselves. You made it about our company, our needs, our concerns . . . I could tell you were here to help."

Inspiration struck like lightening. I got up the courage to ask a second question: "What do you like and dislike about salespeople? Tell me about some of the great and awful experiences you have had with them?" The flood gates opened, and the sales seas parted. I soon realized that I was on to something. I strongly believe that perception is reality, and at a young age, I realized my customers' perception of salespeople was their reality.

Perception . . . could this be the key to your sales growth and relationship building?

I made a commitment to myself to take this to heart, internalize it, and then do the complete opposite of what was shared with me. I took all the negative aspects I was told, which was a long laundry list, and flipped it on its head. I simply did the complete opposite. As silly as it sounds, this was not rocket science, and soon my sales career started to take off.

What's Holding You Back?

What emotional sales baggage from the past has a stranglehold on you? What sales stories are still haunting you that have been left unaddressed? What is holding you back from becoming the best version of yourself as a sales professional?

Will you give yourself permission to take the adventure with me?

Throughout our journey together, the inner work you are willing to do on yourself will fuel the outer success you crave.

Jim Rohn said it best:

Work harder on yourself than you do on your job.

It is all about building trust, but the journey starts with knowing your authentic self.

When I think of trustworthiness, these words come to mind: aboveboard, believable, ethical, honest, honorable, forthright, righteous, dependable. By now, I think you may be sensing where I am going with this. Can these words be used to characterize you, and furthermore, would your clients use these words to describe you?

Trust is built through daily and consistent action. To quote my dear friend, Jack Hubbard:

Authenticity without action is worthless. To know thyself is to value thyself, and this all starts with self-awareness.

What story have you been telling yourself? The stories that play out in our mind become the narratives of our lives. Then, we present that story to our clients and future clients.

Extraordinary sales professionals are those who emphasize their strengths and use them energetically as their self-expression shines through within their business conversations and client interactions.

Lead with the Heart and Trust Others

A genuine professional is all heart. Lead yourself with courage and empathy. This only comes from listening to your heart. These are the skills you need to succeed; they include compassion, kindness, and understanding of others. Consider what it feels like to walk in other's shoes.

When you lead with your heart, you are willing to show vulnerability. We know that to foster trust, you must first trust others. By trusting others first, you reveal vulnerability. When you develop mutual trust, it becomes easier to share ideas, engage in conversation, build upon the relationship, and further grow sales.

To quote Tony Robbins,

The only person who is truly holding you back is you.
No more excuses. It is time to change. It is time to live
life at a new level.

Let's face reality: we are our own worst enemies. When it comes to growth, we are the ones placing shackles on ourselves. I will be the first to admit, stand up, and shout, "I am the one who has stunted my growth over the years."

The stories in our head become the stories of our lives. It is these narratives that play out in our daily lives and cause us to point fingers, play the blame game, and deflect responsibility onto other people when we fail to reach our goals.

Could you be the one holding yourself back from achieving sales success because of what you believe?

We all know that growth and comfort do not play well together and never will.

One word sums up *Selling from the Heart*: authenticity. Until you learn to truly embrace your authentic self, stare down what holds you back, and solve the internal challenges that the little voice inside your head avoids, you will struggle to move forward and achieve the life you envision.

The first step in uncovering what may be holding you back starts with personal accountability and honesty.

> ## Weak salespeople point fingers and deflect, while sales professionals find out what they did wrong and fix it.

Sales professionals build a strong sense of self, based upon personal accountability and these three things:

➢ They do not blame others.
➢ They are consistently looking in the mirror.
➢ They always work on their process.

What prevents sales reps from becoming sales professionals? Mental gymnastics play a huge part in all of this. The sales profession is tough. It wreaks havoc on your confidence, your messaging, and your self-worth.

Combine this with excuses, fear, ego, and undealt-with emotional baggage, and this becomes a recipe for self-destruction.

Excuses

Sales professionals slam the door on excuses because excellence is the key to unlocking their success.

Today, a culture of excuse-making and finger-pointing has replaced disciplined work, boldness, and determination. Many in sales use excuses to rationalize their actions regarding their circumstances, their actions toward other people, and the events or stories that prevent them from hitting their numbers.

Excuse-making is pure B.S. and becomes the primary reason why salespeople are unable to accomplish what they need to succeed. To smash your sales targets, you must take personal responsibility.

It is no one else's responsibility to help you achieve your goals; it is yours and yours alone. This means that if you have a sub-par month and fail to meet your plan, it is not your manager's fault, your customers' fault, or your prospects' fault—it is your fault!

Suck it up buttercup, self-reflect, buckle down, and get to work. Look at yourself in the mirror and commit to getting better.

> **Stop excusing your failures or your procrastination, and start taking the steps necessary to become a sales professional.**

Fear

Your success depends greatly on your skillset, which includes driving profitability, bringing in new business, and client retention.

What is concerning is the amount of salespeople who lack confidence with their sales abilities and skillset. Whose fault is that? Look in the mirror and answer the question honestly. I would say that the lack of practice, preparation, and planning has something to do with one's low skill set.

Based on observation, it is no surprise that many tenured salespeople are nervous, afraid, and hesitant to do anything relevant to improving their sales skillset. The reason is the fear of being exposed!

Admitting one's weakness is no easy step, but it is a step in the right direction.

You must become vulnerable and develop the courage to help overcome your fears.

Vulnerability will set you free because fear of being exposed will keep you in a state of complacency. I believe you can do it. Becoming vulnerable with yourself will not hurt you. It may put in a dent in your pride, but I promise you that it is well worth it.

Set aside the fear, and become vulnerable by:

➢ Asking for help.
➢ Admitting to yourself that you do not know everything.
➢ Embracing the chaos and the stories in your mind.

Ego

Sales professionals must check their ego at the door.

Social media, the movies, and a vast majority of the public portray salespeople as egomaniacs with slick-backed hair and a "do whatever it takes to close the sale" mentality. Perception is reality, and it sure does remind us of *Glengarry Glen Ross* scenes, doesn't it?

While there is always some truth to stereotypes, the biggest exceptions to the rule lie within us.

A huge ego is a sales growth buzzkill.

Ego certainly plays a part in one's success, but it can also hinder one from significant growth. In our highly connected, digitally driven, and socially empowered business world, an assertive, know-it-all mentality combined with a super-charged ego will be the kiss of death in the sales profession.

The real-deal sales professionals—the true superstars—sell from the heart. They are open-minded, curious, collaborative, vulnerable, open to learning, and aim for genuine partnerships with their clients. These professionals have humility and operate without any deception whatsoever. This is a direct conflict to the behavior of ego-driven salespeople.

Being a self-serving ego-maniac ruins relationships, cuts you off from authentic experiences, and chips away at your clients' happiness.

Emotional Baggage

Welcome to the world of the emotional baggage sales club. Sales is stressful and filled with anxieties, worries, inner criticisms, and negative thoughts, especially when we are not hitting our numbers.

Emotional baggage and negative emotions wreak havoc on our mental state. I am waving my hands high in the air right now, as this is an area that has weighed heavily on my heart for decades.

Negative and traumatic past experiences create a prison in our mind, but we must overcome them to grow and attain mental peace, clarity, and sales success. Emotional baggage is like lugging around 50-lb. ankle weights 24/7. It causes insecurities mixed with mental prevention due to events that have taken place in one's life.

This baggage could stem from, for example, a horrific sales manager, an event that happened during a sales meeting, a tough prospecting call, a difficult situation with a customer, or a toxic sales culture.

What baggage from the past may be holding you back? All of this causes trust erosion with respect to others and ourselves. You have a choice. You can continue to hold onto what is holding you back and keeping you from being your best self, or you can choose to work on them one by one.

It does not have to be this way. As we start this journey, I encourage you to find some alone time. Find a place with no distractions, phone, or social media, and have a serious conversation with yourself.

To help you with this process, I encourage you to check out the Trust Formula Mini-Course at www.sellinginaposttrustworld.com.

In the next chapter, we will take a deeper look at the inner work required to let go of all the excuses, fear, ego, and emotional baggage.

Chapter 1 Summary

1. When you change yourself, you start to view your sales life in a different manner. It is all about changing yourself to become a better individual. This, in turn, will make the business world a better place.
2. What happened next started my journey from salesperson to sales professional. They said, "You were the only salesperson who didn't make it about their company, their product, or themselves; you made it about our company, our needs, our concerns...I could tell you were here to help."
3. What emotional sales baggage from the past has a stranglehold on you? What sales stories are still haunting you that have been left unaddressed? What is holding you back from becoming the best version of yourself as a sales professional?
4. When you lead with your heart, you are willing to show vulnerability. We know that to foster trust, you must first trust others. By trusting others first, you display your vulnerability. When you develop mutual trust, it becomes easier to share ideas, engage in conversation, build upon the relationship, and further grow sales.
5. **Stop excusing your failures or your procrastination, and start taking the steps necessary to become a sales professional.**

Chapter 2:

Being Real with Yourself

Kevin hadn't been happy about his sales career for a considerable amount of time, and it sure did show with his lackluster results. Could this morning become the difference-maker? After showering, he found himself locking eyes with someone in the mirror. Was this the same old Kevin, or was this a new Kevin?

Out of his left ear, he faintly heard "Man in the Mirror" by Michael Jackson being played on his favorite 1980s radio station. "How appropriate," he thought to himself.

Normally, he would have blown this off, gotten up, and gone on with his day. Today, though, was a far cry from that. A good friend had been dropping pearls of wisdom and concepts around *Selling from the Heart*, and this got Kevin thinking.

For years, he had been playing the "sales game", and it left him feeling inauthentic and empty. Yes, he was able to achieve periods of success, but it took a tremendous amount of work both mentally and physically.

It was this inconsistency that led him to continually turn over new rocks as frustration set in. Finding new opportunities became tiring, wearing on his soul.

His friend had monumental success and people loved him. Kevin always thought he was weak because he deeply cared about his clients and was not afraid to be himself around them, but now, he was not so sure.

Kevin stared at himself more closely, and what he saw disturbed him. His face showed it. The outline became apparent. All these years, he had been wearing a mask. "What if there was something to what his friend said?" he thought to himself. His friend had suggested the first step was acknowledging the need to change. The second step was committing to do the inner work for his authentic self to shine and come alive. Kevin threw his hands up in the air and shouted, "I am ready." It was at that moment that he made the promise to himself.

As he left for work, he felt lighter than he had in years. He could not wait to speak with his friend to share what was in his heart and to find out the next step.

Where Do You Begin?

In the last chapter, we dove into the importance of doing the inner work and addressing the things that may be holding you back. Recognizing the need to change is the first step towards becoming the sales professional you were meant to be. In this chapter, we will begin the process.

To grow, you must be willing to accept change. This is simple for some, yet so difficult for many. My question for you is,

How are you self-managing change?

According to TransformingEducation.org, self-management can be defined as, "The ability to regulate one's emotions, thoughts, and behaviors effectively in different situations."

Let's look at this through a sales-centric lens. Self-management correlates to understanding your personal responsibility in different aspects of your sales life, and then fulfilling that responsibility.

The question then becomes:

Are you doing what is required to fulfill your sales responsibility to your company and yourself?

I firmly believe that to rise above all the empty suits, you must break bad sales habits. These habits are simply behaviors impacting the decisions you make about how to spend your time, activities, and resources.

From the most tenured of salespeople to the least experienced, recognizing what is a good versus a bad habit is the first critical step in understanding why you do certain things while avoiding other things, such as prospecting.

I wholeheartedly believe that deeply rooted within bad sales habits is a complete lack of personal accountability.

Poor performance is due to bad habits.

What are your bad sales habits? I know, this is not something you want to admit to yourself, but they are there. At what point do these habits begin sabotaging your productivity, performance, your pipeline, and more importantly, your client relationships? How long will you let this go on before you are willing to make the commitment to yourself to put in the time and do the work necessary to become a true sales professional?

Your vision will become clear only when you look into your heart. Who looks outside, dreams; who looks inside, awakens.
Carl Jung

My challenge to the entire sales world is the following: if we can bring our hearts to our personal relationships, then what prevents us from bringing heart to our professional ones?

Embracing a heart-centered approach rests with your ability to stop, look inward, and reflect upon the course of action you know is right, rather than succumbing to external pressures and misaligned sales nonsense that, quite frankly, does not work.

Selling from the Heart goes against everything that standard sales training teaches you. The world has changed, and yet, how we sell seems to be stuck in the dark ages. I believe that everything in life happens from the inside/out. Often, the struggles many have in sales can be correlated to misalignment between the head and the heart.

Are you pouring your mind and soul into your career? If you're struggling to answer this question, then rest assured, you're not alone.

It is hard to sell from the heart if your heart is broken. This is deep, I know, but if you want to transform your sales results and your client relationships, then you must be willing to transform *yourself*.

Look Inward

The journey to healing your heart and growing your sales at an exponential rate starts with understanding who you are at your core. It is about becoming more in tune with your deeper self. It is the ability to recognize what fires you up, what takes you down, and what makes you happy or sad; then, take personal responsibility for the results you achieve.

You cannot blame others when things go wrong. You must be willing to look inward and determine what you could have done to make the outcome better. It is not about blame, but self-examination. You should be able to take a true look at yourself, congratulating yourself on what you did right, and growing stronger in the areas where you are weak.

Are you avoiding facing your own sales soul? If so, ask yourself the following questions:

- ➢ How do you deal with your emotions?
- ➢ How do you react when your sales life goes astray?
- ➢ What areas do you really excel at?
- ➢ What areas do you need to work on in your personal growth and development?

When you truly understand who you are, you will then start to make a conscious effort to improve yourself, creating stronger habits, and communicating with clients and potential clients in a new way. I promise you that this will have an impact on your sales growth.

Here lies the question:

> ## Do you have the courage to bring your heart to your sales life?

Sales professionals actively think about the things they do. They objectively evaluate themselves on a regular basis. They look at things through an unbiased and clear set of lenses.

Daily, they ask themselves:

➤ Am I learning from my mistakes?
➤ Am I consistently pushing myself out of my comfort zone?
➤ Do I still believe that I can do this?

When you can ask yourself these deep questions, then you are starting to look inward.

Generally, as a sales society, we are largely fixated on the outer work. We focus on stack rankings, where we are at quarter or year to date, key performance indicators, and number of new clients. Let's take a step back and realize that these are merely outer symbols. This does not reflect your inner world.

> ## The key to sales happiness lies in transforming yourself and your career through the inner work you do. Do you have the courage to dig in and ask yourself deep questions?

The Inner Work Defines You

What makes your heart sing? How would you define yourself? I encourage you to be your own Sherlock Holmes, and become interested in what grabs your attention and tugs on your heartstrings. Stop looking in the dictionary for words that define you. The world can never tell you who you are.

Getting to know yourself is the truth that allows you to tap into the road called happiness. This is critical to your success as a sales professional. Understanding yourself is about recognizing your shortcomings and putting them on display for others to see and judge.

Yes, this means getting extremely vulnerable. It starts with looking in the mirror and saying to yourself, "This is me. This is the real me. This is who I am."

In turn, if you struggle to ask yourself deep questions, then how will you be able to ask your clients the deep questions that are necessary to build strong relationships?

Become Comfortable with Being Uncomfortable

Becoming comfortable with being uncomfortable is what ferocious self-honesty is built upon. I encourage you to think long about this question:

> **How can you become ferociously self-honest if you struggle to deal with any discomfort in your sales life?**

Those of you who are willing to take risks, step out of your comfort zone, and create some discomfort will reap the biggest rewards.

Let this question sink in for a moment:

> **If you cannot challenge yourself to improve, then how can you challenge your clients to improve?**

John Simone nails it:

The key to wisdom is knowing all the right questions.

The questions you ask yourself reflect the sales life you lead. This determines what your mind focuses on, which triggers certain thoughts, actions, and inactions, ultimately affecting your sales results.

When you can ask yourself empowering, deeply reflective questions, it shifts your mind to a whole new level and sets into motion the thinking and actions to jumpstart your sales life.

What Happens When the Emotional Blocks Are Removed

Reflect on this quote from James Allen:

The outer conditions of a person's life will always reflect their inner beliefs.

When you learn how to smash the cinderblocks that have been weighing you down, the pressure comes off. You feel freer and more alive, and you can be real and lead the sales life you so desperately crave. I firmly believe that when you get rid of all the mental trash and blocks holding you back, it allows you to become beacons of hope for your clients and future clients.

A beacon is a source of light and inspiration. Do your clients and potential clients see you that way? When you walk into their company or join them on a virtual meeting, does their face light up? Do they lean into your conversations, or lean back in your conversations?

Every day, you have endless opportunities to become a beacon.

> ➢ You become a beacon every time you get through a challenging conversation with a client.
> ➢ You become a beacon every time you stretch yourself by speaking the truth.
> ➢ You become a beacon every time you take off the mask and allow yourself to be real.

Be that beacon of inspiration for your clients. Become the lighthouse, and guide them towards business betterment. This only happens when you remove the head trash and the junk in the trunk of your heart.

When you can be straight with your clients, they will be straight with you.

I encourage you to live your sales life as a BEACON of hope:

B: Belief
E: Encouragement
A: Attitude
C: Compassion
O: Offer to help
N: Nourish

Guess what happens when you become a beacon? Others are drawn to you. They may not even know why they are. Light always dispels the darkness. You could be in an enormous pitch-black concert arena, and one person turns the flashlight on their phone and then proceeds to hold it up; soon, everyone there will instantly see it and be drawn to the light. Become that light in a dark place.

I am excited about the next chapter as we take the inner work you have just begun and use it to start transforming your sales career. The inner work only counts if you allow others to see it.

Chapter 2 Summary

1. If you cannot challenge yourself to improve, then how can you challenge your clients to improve?
2. In turn, if you struggle to ask yourself deep questions, then how will you be able to ask your clients the deep questions that are necessary to build strong relationships?
3. The key to sales happiness lies in transforming yourself and your career through the inner work you do.
4. Are you doing what is needed to fulfill your sales responsibility to your company and yourself?
5. I encourage you to live your sales life as a BEACON of hope:

B: Belief
E: Encouragement
A: Attitude
C: Compassion
O: Offer to help
N: Nourish

Chapter 3:

Being Real with Others

Samantha sat comfortably in her office patiently waiting for her next appointment, a sales rep named Christian. "Oh no, here we go again," she thought to herself, "Another sales rep who is going to look at me as a woman and think I am either a soft pushover, or I can be charmed into saying 'yes'."

This was *the* one huge aspect of her job that she despised: molding and grooming a new sales rep, with the outcome of getting him to respect her.

After a subtle tap on the door, Samantha sat straight up, making herself look as tall as possible. "Come on in." Christian casually walked in, shook her hand, politely said hello, then sat down, pausing and waiting for her to start the conversation.

Immediately, this caught her attention. Normally, all the other sales reps would go first attempting to gain the upper hand. Samantha become keenly aware of how well Christian was dressed: professionally, but not pretentious.

"Tell me a little bit about yourself, Christian," she began. What came next caught Samantha totally off-guard. He did not brag about his accomplishments, but openly shared real moments about his life and career, then asked about hers.

The conversation effortlessly continued, switching from personal to business. Through it all, though, Christian stayed true to himself and treated her with the utmost of respect. As the meeting came to an end, Samantha knew she could trust Christian. She then proceeded to schedule another future date on her calendar for Christian to meet the rest of her team. As Christian left, Samantha said to herself, "Finally, a sales professional and not another empty, all-about-me sales rep."

Trust Is the Key

Trust is built when we are real. Being real and transparent in sales is nonnegotiable. In a business world full of emptiness, transparency and realness is an absolute must. People sense BS, facades, and insincerity instantaneously.

When you can become transparent and real, this forms the foundational layers of trust, which in turn, creates the basis for loyal relationships. Without loyalty, you are a mere commodity. Without being real, you will be viewed as just another sales rep.

Jonathan Harnisch nails it:

Forget about being impressive and commit to being real. Because being real is impressive.

What's Your Secret Sauce?

Being real in world full of sales facades is a gift.

In today's fast-paced business environment, people are crazy busy, multitasking, and pressed for time. The use of technology has exploded. It has become challenging to interact on a one-to-one basis. We used to go see someone in person, or at least pick up the phone; now, we may go months upon months only communicating by text, email, or social platforms.

Faceless communication is a rampant sales epidemic; what are you doing about it?

What is the greatest gift you can give your clients, your future clients, and those in your marketplace? The greatest gift you can give is the real *you*!

In true *Selling from the Heart* fashion, I would like for you to think about giving your clients time, attention, love, caring, and compassion.

If you are not spending time with your clients and not digging into their business initiatives, goals, or desires, then stop and think: who may be? When you can give the gift of yourself, it comes across as: "You're extremely important to me. I care about you, and you are valuable."

Andrew Carnegie once said,

> *Here is the prime condition of success, the great secret—concentrate your energy, thought, and capital exclusively upon the business in which you are engaged. Having begun on one line, resolve to fight it out on that line, to lead in it, adopt every improvement, have the best machinery, and know the most about it. The concerns which fail are those which have scattered their capital, which means that they have scattered their brains also.*

Andrew Carnegie become a billionaire because he refused to let his resources scatter across a thousand different things. He concentrated everything he had—his thoughts, energy, and capital—on one single thing.

For me, my single mission is creating a movement to bring back sincerity, substance, and heart to the sales profession. Many have drifted off the true path. Whether you are in leadership, management, or in sales, I encourage you to think about this one thing:

What's the one gift you can bring to your clients and prospects that will set you apart?

Your clients deserve more. You know they do, and I know they do. The question becomes: what will you do about it? Your gift just might be the best present you can give to your clients. I encourage all of you to give the most inexpensive and yet most precious gift there is: *you*.

You may not think much of yourself as a gift and, heck, you may not even feel that you have much to give, but I am here to tell you that you do have a gift.

Let's unite, as it is time to uncover it.

Uncover Your Gift

I am a massive Steve Harvey fan. I enjoy his humor, his style, and what he believes in. When it comes to thinking about your gift, consider the following:

Your whole life will have new meaning and direction when you recognize your gift and decide upon the most valuable way to use it.
Steve Harvey

If you are not sure what your gift is, ask yourself these three questions:

- ➢ What can I do that I am the best at, and with little effort on my part?
- ➢ What is the one thing that other people associate with me?
- ➢ I have listened to others connect this gift with me, so how have I used it?

Each one of you are sitting on a treasure trove of collective gifts. Are you capitalizing on those gifts? *Selling from the Heart* professionals capitalize on their gifts.

If you are still struggling with your secret sauce, I am here to say it's okay. It may take you some time to uncover it, but rest assured that you will.

Here are three gifts you can give to your clients and future clients.

The Gift of Gratitude

Showing gratitude can change every aspect of your life. Gratitude rarely comes naturally. It is something that we need to *choose* to do, and it *must* be intentional and come right from the heart!

Are you grateful for your clients? Right now, take out a sheet of paper. Write down ten reasons why you are grateful for your clients. I know this might be difficult, but I promise you that it is well worth the effort.

Once completed, I encourage you to share these with your clients. My promise is that this will forever change the course of your relationship with them. Heartfelt professionals know that without any clients, they have no business.

Gratitude can be the simplest cure for a lack of motivation.

The Gift of Vulnerability

Vulnerability is scary. However, it may be the greatest gift that you can give to yourself and your clients. We often go about protecting ourselves by building walls around us, failing to show our clients our fears or insecurities. True human connection lies beneath the surface. It is being able to show vulnerability that makes us stronger.

Through vulnerability, we can connect with our clients in the deepest of ways. This takes courage! If you really want to connect with your clients, then stop the charades, dig in, rip the mask off, and become vulnerable. Heartfelt professionals embrace vulnerability, as they know this bridges the relational gaps.

The Gift of Connection

Connecting with your clients is vital. You must make them feel like you truly care, and this means you should stop looking at them through your dollar-signed glasses.

We as human beings want to be heard. We want to know that we matter, and we want to be loved (or even just liked). When we feel accepted, we perform better. We become a bit more relaxed, and we do not come across as being insecure. Can you relate? The same can be said about your clients as well.

Heartfelt conversations lead to a human connection. Heartfelt professionals are present in the moment. Your clients should be made to feel like they are the only thing that matters. Speak from your heart. Most people can tell when you are being sincere or faking it. When you start communicating with authenticity, you'll find that the trust and relatability factors soar.

When was the last time you shared with one of your clients how you really felt?

Sharing Your Gift

Each one of you has a certain special gift that is unique to you. There is no one else in the world with that gift, and you need to share it. This gift is something that comes easily and naturally to you.

Uncovering your gift might be the best present you can give to yourself and to your clients.

How Are You Humanizing Yourself and Your Client Relationships?

Without engagement, your gift, and human connection, how will you grow your sales and your client relationships?

In this technology crazed, socially connected, and digitally driven business world, how well are you truly connecting to your clients? It becomes painfully difficult to bring the real *you* to the forefront while hiding behind technology.

Highly successful sales professionals have extremely valuable networks that they have developed, nurtured, and invested a considerable amount of time in maintaining them.

We are social creatures, hard-wired to seek out a community. In fact, our drive for human connection is so powerful that multiple studies have shown that feeling lonely and isolated is more detrimental to our health than smoking or obesity.

I ask all of you to think about the following: If you build a large and smart network, never engaging in conversation, then is that not the equivalent of compiling a massive Rolodex and never reaching out to anyone?

> **Networking—whether done intentionally or coincidentally—can create a huge competitive advantage for you.**

Anything you wish to accomplish in sales requires people. Even if you are an amazing sales professional, without an active network, you will struggle to consistently succeed.

> **To connect, you must share and ask for others to share.**

I am here to inform all of you who have big social followings and tons of connections on LinkedIn that you must engage with your following and connections. Think of it as providing big social media hugs. You must include an in-person, human component and feel. This is how you build social credibility. You never know when you will need it, but when you do, it is heavenly!

If you do not have the network or fail to build one, you are missing one key ingredient: people. Without people, there is no one to spread the word about you!

I am concerned that the human connection has been lost in sales. Human connection is the energy exchange between people who are paying attention to one another.

Are you paying attention to your clients and future clients?

You have the power to deepen the connection, inspire change, and build trust. My question to you is: are you committed to humanizing yourself?

It's More Than Clicking Connect

You have heard the saying, "Your network is your net worth." However, building a network takes more than simply clicking a "connect" button on LinkedIn. It requires consistent active engagement.

A *Selling from the Heart* professional brings their heart to their network. They know it is okay to bring their genuine, authentic, and real-deal self as they throw their arms around their network.

When you add authenticity and heart to your network, watch what happens and who engages back. Build a love fest with your network. Do it because you care. When it comes to the power of connection, Richard Branson stated,

> *A confident person will try to improve the relationship; an arrogant person will try to prove themselves.*

One will never know when they'll need their network. Therefore, sales professionals consistently educate their network.

In Chapter 1 of one of my favorite books, *Not Taught*, by Jim Keenan, he refers to the reach revolution:

> *It's never been easier to market to, connect with, and engage anyone, anywhere in the world in real time—that is, instantly. Like it or not, the business world has gone global, and the shift has created the greatest new opportunity for success ever.*

How are you creating your own reach revolution?

The power of social media is about human engagement. Start engaging, educating, and humanizing your network. Become diligent and invest in your network daily. Do this intentionally, and do it in an authentic manner.

Unfortunately, the digital world has made many in sales lazy. One cannot hide behind a keyboard forever! A heartfelt professional drives conversation, leaves an impression, adds value, and builds relationships. They truly tug on the heart strings of their network.

Your network is built over time.

To build a true digital connection, one must engage and invest. Why? Because when you need your network, it is there. They will rally and rise to the occasion to help. How do you expect it to grow if you do not invest in it? What impression are you leaving within your network? You will get out of your network what you put into it.

A 401k Human Network

Consistent deposits in your retirement funds allows you to live a fruitful life in your golden years. Are you making consistent deposits with your network? Are you building a network of people who know you? Are you diversifying your network? Are you adding value to their lives? Does your network know the real you? Are you masquerading online as one person, but offline you are someone else?

Invest in your network, humanize it, and bring it to life. You are one degree of separation away from your best sales opportunity. Unfortunately, many fail to realize this because they fail to connect the social network dots.

You can truly leverage your network into an "engine of wealth."

Don't get me wrong; technology is wonderful, and it runs rampant in the twenty-first century, but we must not forget to humanize it. Many in sales are leveraging technology in order to make those connections stronger and deeper.

> **A heartfelt professional leverages technology to humanize their network.**

Think about combining technology and the "digital you" together to humanize what you are all about. Your network will feel it and see it; most of all, your network will live it with you. There's incredible power behind genuine engagement with other human beings to drive sales success.

Proximity is power. If you can get proximity with people that are the best in the world, things can happen because all of the people they know, the insights they

have, and the life experience they have. They can save
you a decade of time by one insight.
Tony Robbins

If you have a burning desire to grow, then ask yourself, who are you hanging out with? If you want to professionally grow, then think about this insight from Tony Robbins:

If you want to turn your goals into reality faster, then
get yourself in proximity with people who are playing
the game at a higher level than you do.

You become who you hang around with! How many people have found their pathway to success or simply lost it, all because of the friends they keep or the people they mingle with? Think about how this applies to you and your sales career.

This old quote applies to all:

Birds of the same feather flock together.

Ultimately, the company you keep has the power to influence and change you.

Who Is Influencing Your Sales Growth?

Your friends and circle of influence will:

➢ Impact you indirectly with what they do.
➢ Impact you directly by teaching and giving you advice.

Stephen M.R. Covey in his classic book, *The 7 Habits of Highly Effective People*, explains that truly effective people who expand their influence live a life focused on things that they can change—their circle of influence—and not things they have no power over, which can be categorized in a circle of concern.

Covey goes on to say,

> *Proactive people focus their efforts in the Circle of Influence. They work on the things they can do something about. The nature of their energy is positive, enlarging and magnifying, causing their Circle of Influence to increase.*

Are you proactive in your efforts when it comes to building your circle of influence within your professional career?

Within your client base, who is in your circle of influence? Imagine a tight-knit influential circle of clients from various levels all coming together for business betterment—yours and theirs.

What could that do for your professional growth and business success? Who is lifting you up, and who might be tearing you down within your inner circle? The standards you have for yourself, your business, and the people you associate with must be high, continually elevating you to grow.

Surround yourself with people who lift you up, lend you their knowledge and connections, and are strong enough to help you learn from your mistakes.

> **The key to your sales growth comes directly through the circle of influence you build with your current clients.**

At some point in your career, you have heard some version of the Jim Rohn's quote, "You're the average of the five people you spend most of your time with."

The truth is that who you spend the most time with is who you eventually become.

As we close out this chapter, I encourage you to head on over to www.sellinginaposttrustworld.com and check out the free resources. Here, you will discover tools to help you think through what you read as you implement it into your life.

Chapter 3 Summary

1. Trust is built when we are real. Being real and transparent in sales is nonnegotiable. People sense BS, facades, and insincerity instantaneously.
2. Being real in a world full of sales facades and empty suits is a gift and the secret sauce that makes all the difference.
3. If you are not sure what your gift is, ask yourself these three questions:

   ➢ What can I do that I am the best at, and with little effort on my part?
   ➢ What is the one thing that other people associate with me?
   ➢ I have listened to others connect this gift with me, so how have I used it?

4. If nothing else, you can always give the gift of gratitude, vulnerability, and connection.
5. In this technology-crazed, socially connected, and digitally driven business world, how well are you truly connecting to your clients? It becomes painfully difficult to bring the real you to the forefront while hiding behind technology.
6. Are you proactive in your efforts when it comes to building your circle of influence within your professional career?

Chapter 4:

Your Community Matters

If you want to go fast, go alone.
If you want to go far, go with others.
African Proverb

t's quite a journey we've been on in a short period of time. How are you holding up?

Together, we have examined what it means to be your true authentic self.

I believe you will struggle to serve your clients if who you are in the mirror does not match the reflection that others see.

You learned how excuses, fear, ego, and emotional baggage hold you back, keeping the empty suit syndrome alive. You learned that by looking inward, you can let that all go, as you allow others to see you for who you are.

Lastly, we have unwrapped the gifts within yourself and how you can use them to serve your clients, cementing even stronger relationships.

The underlying factor throughout all of this is trust. Developing deep layers of trust is the foundation that relationships are based upon. This becomes the bedrock on which trusted client communities are formed.

Rest assured on this one! Building rock-solid trusted client communities will become the launching pad for sales growth and an endless source of referrals.

The Right Type of Clients Matter

Look no further than your client relationships—these are the people you engage with the most.

Let's pause for a moment, as I would like for you to reflect upon the following:

- ➢ What kind of energy are your clients bringing you?
- ➢ What can you learn from them?
- ➢ How do they support you?
- ➢ How do you feel after spending time with them?

If you find yourself in a quandary, then I must ask: are you aligning with the right type of clients?

Your clients should bring out the best in you. If they are bringing out the worst in you, then this is a serious red flag that they may not be the right fit.

I would like you to grab your client list, and ask yourself, "Are these the right type of clients, and do I have the right kind of relationships?"

- ➢ What do you *really know about them?*
- ➢ *What do they really know about you?*
- ➢ *What circles of influence do they associate with?*

The more you invest in your client relationships, the more you can collect from your client relationships.

Proximity to Power and Influence Is Priceless

Think about all the decision-makers and influencers within your client base. Are you putting yourself in proximity to the people that they know?

I believe you are one degree of separation and one relationship away from your best sales opportunity. Who are you putting yourself in proximity to?

In digging into the notion of proximity through the lens of *Wikipedia*, I discovered the "Proximity Principle."

Theodore Newcomb, an American social psychologist, professor, and author, was the first to document the effects of proximity on acquaintance and attraction. He first documented this effect through his study of the acquaintance process, which demonstrated how people who interact and live close to each other will be more likely to develop a relationship.

> *Tell me who your friends are,*
> *and I'll tell you who you are.*
> **Don Quixote by Miguel de Cervantes**

Applying the Proximity Principle to your clients, I must ask you again, how often are you putting yourself in proximity to your clients and to the people they know?

One of the best ways to grow your sales is to have a greater impact, master influence, and add more value to your clients. Simply surround yourself with people who have the power to support your vision, product, and services.

Proximity to power is the ability to surround yourself with influence. These are people who can help elevate your activities by simply making one phone call, one introduction, or a recommendation.

Who are the influencers you are surrounding yourself with? Are they people who can direct traffic towards your business? If you are struggling to answer, then maybe it is time to start surrounding yourself with influential players.

I encourage you to push the boundaries and get uncomfortable. Meet and surround yourself with bigger players, power players, and the prestigious, and then watch how sales magic starts to happen.

You have heard this before: who you hang out with you soon become.

As my dear friend and coach, Dave Sanderson, often says, "It's about building the right associations and taking massive action on it."

Without action, your sales results will dwindle.

Understanding Your Community Network

Your various clients have at least one thing in common: you. Conversely, many have other things in common, such as job title, corporate challenges, hobbies, and possibly even life experiences.

What would it be like if you became the connector, the relational bridge-builder, and the conduit to all of them that, in turn, brings real value?

Regarding community in a sales context, let's use the following definition from the *Oxford English Dictionary*:

> *A feeling of fellowship with others, as a result of sharing common attitudes, interests, and goals.*

Here lies two questions for many of you:

- ➢ Are you creating fellowship with your clients?
- ➢ What common interests and goals do you have with your clients?

I believe to build real community with your clients, not only do you need to care about community, but you also need to care about and respect each other.

You need to be loyal to one another and build healthy relationships. Creating a community around you, the real *you*, requires work. However, the road taken to grow one will have ever-lasting benefits for a long time to come.

Heartfelt Sales Professionals Build Community

Dean Ornish nails it when he says,

> *The need for connection and community is primal, as fundamental as the need for air, water, and food.*

In the crazy, challenging, and competitive world of sales, how do you stand out from all the other salespeople who do the exact same thing as you?

Heartfelt professionals future-proof their business and reputation through the communities they build with their clients. This is their competitive advantage! This is how they grow their sales.

I encourage you to gather your clients together for harmonious feedback, listen to what they are working on, listen to their challenges, uncover their vision, and foster an environment to openly share ideas. Client communities can also help you to see your product, business, or industry from the perspective of the very same people you are selling to.

By continually communicating in a transparent and personal way with your clients, you will improve trust, belief, and faith.

> **In a post-trust sales world, building client communities bridges the relational divide.**

Could an unfiltered communication channel with your clients help to strengthen relationships? You bet it will! Your clients will start to feel heard, recognized, and rewarded; from there, trust will grow exponentially.

Developing client communities helps cultivate connections and comradery between like-minded individuals. For example, consider developing a financial community, a technology community, a human resource community, and a leadership community, to name a few. Now, think about harnessing the collective knowledge of these communities to foster collaborative learning environments.

In doing so, you have now created environments to openly share thoughts, wants, ideas, dreams, visions, and aspirations.

Building community brings your clients together to meet like-minded peers, to further their knowledge, and to feel more positively and more connected to you. Most of all, this is a place with no added noise, no ads, and no social media algorithms.

Everyone Benefits

Envision for a moment a client community that shares things in common, cares deeply about each other, and works closely together for betterment or a purpose. What kind of harmony could you create from all of this? What do you think all of this does to your client relationships?

Developing community with your clients creates a greater sense of belonging. It powers innovation along with the ability to deliver unique insights, new prospecting ideas, and sales growth opportunities. Isn't this what you want?

Creating a space for your clients to connect and collaborate will facilitate relational growth. More importantly, this creates unique differentiation—and that differentiation is *you*.

As we close out this section, I want to share Carrie McCann's story with you in her own words. This is what building authentic relationships is all about.

Carrie and I initially connected through a video she posted on LinkedIn back in 2017. The minute I started watching the video, I knew Carrie was the real deal. Over the years, we became friends. What has made this relationship so special is that I was blessed to be her coach. We built a powerful friendship based upon open, honest, and trusted conversations.

What I love about Carrie is that she truly cares about what she does. With a giving spirit and true authenticity, Carrie cares about giving back. This is hard to find in sales today, as most salespeople make it about them. Carrie is sincere, genuine, and really places her clients first and foremost above all.

Her story of transformation is powerful and illustrates why the journey to discover what authenticity really means starts with the road to self-discovery.

If I could explain what the past four years were like for me in one phrase, I would choose "What I know today." When I look back at who I was in 2018 compared to where I am now, I don't recognize her. I was either living so far in the past, or so far in the future, that I never embraced what was right in front of me. As I share my story with you, my hope is that something resonates strongly inside: a light bulb moment, or a feeling of relief that what you're sensing inside someone else has experienced too!

Back in 2018, I remember rocking my daughter while she was asleep. I was counting down the days until I could go back to work. I had 500 thoughts in my mind telling me to enjoy maternity leave. This was "supposed to be" the time to bond with your child. I now know that what I was experiencing was silence. Little did I know at the time that life was giving me a "nudge" to WAKE UP! As I found myself going back to work, I still felt like something was missing. The year prior, I had just come off one of my best sales years to date. In my mind, I had more than enough surrounding me to make me happy. Still, why was I struggling so much? Why was something missing?

I remember seeing Larry speak, and it was something he said that hit me at my core: "Why don't you ask your clients what they think of your service?" It was such a simple tip that had so much truth. So, at that point in my life, I needed to understand more. How could such a simple statement ring so much truth for me on the inside. I NEEDED to learn more. I knew it was "a need" vs. "a want" because of that nagging and persistent gut instinct. I took a small step and reached out for sessions with Larry because I had hit my goals and was still unhappy.

I started to learn that when it got quiet, it got uncomfortable. To compensate, I did what I knew best: I worked my butt off and became an F5 tornado. I also knew that I had an addictive personality. It didn't matter if I just had won the largest deal of my life, or hit the worst low of my life, I found ways to numb this feeling. This was the case whether it was going 100 mph or going to the not-so-healthy habit of smoking. This was not sustainable. I knew that if I stayed on this track, I physically wouldn't survive. It was an eerie, deep, and dark feeling of knowing that if I stayed on this course, none of it mattered because my body physically would not be able to handle it.

I took Larry's advice and talked to my clients, asking them about my service. It's natural to want to be seen and validated. It's also natural to have worries and fears. Why did I hesitate so much with getting feedback from my clients? I knew that I was doing a good job, but was I?

The truth can hurt, and sometimes we already know it, but we don't know how to fix it. Does this sound familiar? I had been so busy trying "to be everything for everyone" that I lost sight of what truly mattered. I became stagnant, bored, and out of touch, but my work with Larry showed me that I don't have to be that way.

I hope that my story shows and empowers you that one simple step forward can spark a change in you that you had no idea existed. That spark ignited my passion. When I started to get more "real" with myself and my clients, it led to some of the most meaningful conversations I have ever had. The honesty, transparency, and focus became aligned. When you can get in alignment with your customers, this is when creativity pours, innovation is born, and success is delivered on both sides.

Then, 2020 hit. I've been in sales for nearly twenty years, and this was by far one of THE toughest times mentally in my career. If you were having troubles prior to 2020, it was now magnified with nowhere to go but to face it.

If it weren't for the solid connections and partnerships, I most likely would have struggled with sales after the COVID-19 shutdowns. As you read further with the tools Larry will provide, pick one or two that resonate and take the first small step. These tools will trigger yourself internally on where you need to adjust. This process can be humbling as well.

I had to take a real hard look in the mirror to finally understand that it started with me. I could no longer blame others for things not working out well. I had to take some responsibility and start improving my overall delivery. Just step back and think about a time 10 years ago. I bet you're not the same person. Sometimes, we use the tools we have always had. Some of these tools still work because of the foundation. However, as with any tool, you must modify it to your purposes. Pick and choose the tools that are right for you. This is when you will start to discover your true authentic self.

I want to add a quick message for anyone just starting out in sales. The rejection may be starting to take a toll on you. Remember, all you need is that first small step and "spark" to ignite your vitality. Do what works for you. I had a former employer reach out to me after I had left. He said, "Carrie, you told me you hated to cold call. However, you were the first person ever to show me you can do it differently." There is always a tool and a way; you just have to find the tool that feels right to you. We all have a special talent and gift. You will uncover this gift when you start getting honest and transparent with yourself. Then, your purpose becomes clear, vivid, and sustainable.

Chapter 4 Summary

1. The clients you surround yourself with should bring out the best in you. If they are bringing out the worst in you, then this could be a serious red flag that they may not be the right fit.
2. You are one relationship away from your best deal. Who are you putting yourself in proximity to?
3. Proximity to power is your ability to surround yourself with influence. These are people that can help you elevate your activities by simply making one phone call, one introduction, or a recommendation.
4. What would it be like if you became the connector, the relational bridge-builder, and figured out a way to connect all of them that, in turn, brings real value to them?
5. Heartfelt professionals future-proof their business and reputation through the communities they build with their clients. This is their competitive advantage! This is how they grow their sales.

Section 2 Introduction:

Meaningful Value

Building trust with your clients is paramount for securing referrals, incremental sales growth, cross-selling, and network-strengthening. In a world full of skepticism, suspicion, and doubt, your clients and future clients are asking the question, "Who can I trust?"

People crave transparency and integrity from those they do business with.

To grow, succeed, and flourish, you must have the trust of your clients.

I believe that building trust is foremost. When you commit and make the investment in building, managing, and protecting relationships of trust, performance, conversations, and relational parity all improve. Isn't this what you want?

Many of us are familiar with the age-old saying, "There are two sides of the coin." This can be applied in building trusted relationships with your clients.

On one side of the trust coin, there is authentic relationships, and on the other side, there is meaningful value.

You can build all the relationships in the world with your clients, but without bringing meaningful value, all you will have are a bunch of friends, inconsistent sales, and an upset sales leader. Conversely, if you bring meaningful value, ideas, and insight, but struggle to build those relationships, your sales funnel is going to be rather dry, you will be broke, and you will still have an upset sales leader.

Chapter 5:

Meaningful Value

*Adding value to others is the surest way
to add value to our own lives.*
John C. Maxwell

Anotification window popped up on Greg's CRM screen prompting him he needed to call Fred, the operations manager for a major industrial supplier on his targeted account list. For the past year, Greg called him religiously every two months to share industry-related news while providing any value he could. He enjoyed the conversations, and he knew Fred did as well.

The clock on his monitor displayed it was getting close to the end of the day. Greg knew he could always call Fred tomorrow, but based on past experiences, he was reminded that the things he put off today would somehow be forgotten tomorrow.

So, he picked up his phone, and dialed Fred's number. Immediately, Fred picked it up. "Greg, how did you know I needed to speak with you?" His voice sounded a bit frantic.

"I didn't. We hadn't spoken in months. I was thinking about you and called to say hello. By any chance, would you happen to have a few minutes?"

Fred answered, "I am so glad you called. I just got off the phone with one of my suppliers who informed me that the past few years have taken a toll on their company. Effective immediately, they are shutting down their operations. I can't even place one last order, and their part is an integral component in our product. I know you sell the same part. Can you help me out? I can place an order with you today."

This conversation ensued for the next hour as they worked through the details. Greg knew the product was in the warehouse, and he could get it out to him overnight. The conversation ended with Fred saying, "Thank you so much for your persistence. It was my intent to do business with you last year, as I started to notice inconsistencies with the support I was getting by their sales rep. I was always overruled by my director. Please send me the invoice and I will personally ensure that Accounting processes the invoice immediately. Moving forward, we can then look at setting up payment terms on continual orders. Have a great day Greg, I look forward to doing more business with you." With that, he hung up the phone.

Greg smiled to himself and was so glad he had not put off the call until tomorrow.

Benjamin Franklin once said, "Don't put off until tomorrow what you can do today."

This is a stark reminder: don't put off until tomorrow what you *should* do today.

It Starts with Conversations

You can build all the relationships in the world with your clients, but without showing them the value you bring, they will only view you as a great person to hang around with. On the other side, if you bring great value, but struggle to truly care about them, you become viewed as being just another sales rep.

The glue bringing these two elements together are conversations.

Dale Carnegie said it best,

If you want to be a good conversationalist, be a good listener. To be interesting, be interested.

The way you open conversations has a direct impact on what happens next. The direction of those conversations along with the strategy behind them will all have a direct bearing on one thing: potential sales opportunities.

> **You never know when one conversation will lead to exponential sales growth.**

At this moment in time, how many of you are engaging in real, genuine, and meaningful conversations with your clients? If so, how would you know?

The lack of conversational competence in the sales world concerns me. Far too many are relying on scripted questions yielding scripted answers. All of this resembles a tennis match, and the outcome usually resides with the client 6-0, 6-0 (for all of you tennis aficionados), with the salesperson losing.

Conversations build relationships, and relationships build businesses.

Real conversations require complete participation and you to be present in the moment. Genuine and meaningful conversations are invitations to let the other person share with you what is really going on.

How do you achieve authentic, meaningful, and real conversations with your clients? It's quite simple, yet so difficult: you let your guard down and stop acting like a salesperson.

When salespeople embrace vulnerability, allowing the conversation to flow and enter a realm of uncertainty, the likelihood of genuine engagement skyrockets. How comfortable are you with your clients, so, in return, they become comfortable enough sharing their uncomfortable business concerns?

A real and meaningful conversation is a business adventure into the unknown. This is where you allow the conversation to flow, unscripted and unguarded, and you welcome what you uncover. This is where new possibilities and opportunities to help await you. Are you brave enough to start a conversation that matters?

In his book, *Together: The Healing Power of Human Connection in a Sometimes Lonely World*, American physician and author, Dr. Vivek Murthy, challenges us to ask ourselves questions like:

> *What was it about that conversation? Did I have a break-through moment where I let my guard down? Allowed myself to be vulnerable and was real with the other person? Or was it that they did that with me? And by being vulnerable, they actually empowered me to be the same with them?*

Sales professionals are brave enough to start proactive, meaningful, and value-based conversations that matter. Are you?

What Do Proactive Conversations Look Like?

First, let's examine the difference between reactive and proactive conversations.

Reactive

This is a conversation you may not have planned for, or something that has caused you to respond in an unforeseen manner.

Proactive

With this approach, you prevent problems before they arise. You answer questions before they ask you. You work with your clients, having open conversations around issues important to the both of you.

Sales professionals understand this one thing: proactive conversations are planned, purposeful, and deliver on their promises.

Proactive and real conversations set sales professionals apart from sales reps by creating an environment of trust.

Let's take a look at a few benefits of proactive and real conversations:

- *Shows You Care*

Sales professionals dedicate the additional time to provide insights and creative ideas for their clients to help them grow their business. They do this because they care, as it sets them apart from all the other salespeople.

• *Builds Trust*

In a post-trust sales world, proactive conversation shows you are invested in their business growth. Sales professionals closely monitor their clients' business, and routinely engage with knowledgeable insights to help them cast vision about their business.

• *Prevents Future Issues*

Sales professionals make sure there are no surprises. They know how to prevent their clients from "making a mountain out of a molehill." With proactive conversations, you will gain a better understanding about their needs and possible challenges before they turn into real business issues.

One of the single best resources you have to help you understand your clients' business are your clients. Engage with them; ask them questions; and learn something new about them. What is really going on inside their business? What is going on with them? Imagine what you can discover if you are willing to ask.

One huge benefit of this approach is that what you uncover becomes a conversation starter when prospecting for new clients. The opportunities are endless if you are willing to travel down the conversational road to the unknown.

Sales professionals understand their clients, their business, and their competitive landscape. Are you someone who truly cares about improving your clients' business lives? Do you care about them as people? How can you improve the business lives of your clients? The answer is quite simple: just ask them. *Make it about them.* I cannot stress this enough.

Do you want to get to know your clients? Start with proactive, intentional, and curiosity-driven conversations.

The best way to do that is to leverage triggers to help facilitate the start of your questions. Use phrases such as:

- Tell me more . . .
- Just for a moment, can I get you to put on your thinking cap . . .
- Imagine for a moment, what would happen if . . .

Try inserting these statements into your question starters and watch what happens to your conversations.

Engaging questions lead to engaging conversations, which lead to relationship building whether it be digital, face to face, or via the phone. Proactively engaging in conversations will catapult your sales success.

Are You Creating an Alignment of Value?

I love this quote from John C. Maxwell:

When values, thoughts, feelings, and actions are in alignment, a person becomes focused, and character is strengthened.

I must ask: how much value are you creating for your clients and future clients to help grow your sales and their business? All too often, I hear salespeople, sales management, and those in leadership sing praise to the importance of creating value. Inside a sea of sales sameness, *value* irrefutably becomes one of the single biggest aspects.

However, to build value, we must know its true meaning.

Merriam-Webster defines value as:

- The monetary worth of something.
- A fair return or equivalent in goods, services, or money for something exchanged.
- Relative worth, utility, or importance.
- Something (such as a principle or quality) intrinsically valuable or desirable.

My question is: do you know your worth?

Avoid the Sea of Sameness

Unfortunately, too many in sales act like walking, talking brochures, simply regurgitating product information. Your clients are not buying into your facts and features. They can learn all of this on their own.

Many of your potential clients are not even product-oriented in their thinking. Their focus is on finding a solution to their challenges and problems, or achieving their initiatives. This is what creates value for them. When you pound your chest and rattle off great wizardry about your products, you fail to position yourself and your knowledge as the answer to their business discomfort, frustration, or aspiration.

Instead, all you've done is position yourself as a commodity, swimming in the deep red sales ocean known as the "sea of sameness." Attention, sales community: you have allowed the buyer to base more of their purchasing decision on price, thereby pressuring profit margins as they crush you with the sales sameness hammer.

A true sales professional creates value through the eyes of their clients. With 20/20 vision, they clearly gain the opportunity to be viewed like none other in the marketplace as if they have created a new market segment.

They have dramatically repositioned themselves from their competition. Price now becomes a less dominating factor within the purchasing decision. I get it; at some point, price may become an issue, but if they perceive unique value, then price will never be *the* issue.

> **Creating value not only transforms sales effectiveness, but it also provides insulation from the price hammer.**

How to Start Creating Value

Building strong relationships, and understanding holistically what value means, lays the foundation for becoming valuable. There are three types of value: internal, client, and company value.

Internal Value

A sales professional deeply understands their value. They know that value is deeply cemented within the foundation of their business house.

What makes you valuable?

People will not engage in a business conversation or buy from you if they do not even understand why they should pay attention to you. A sales professional understands that their value statement is their promise. It is the value they deliver, communicate, and are held accountable for fulfilling.

Given client expectations and the competitive business landscape, you must consistently review your value statement as part of your personal business strategy.

I encourage you to spend time with your clients to gain clear knowledge as to whether you are meeting and fulfilling your value statement with them.

On a daily basis, a sales professional will ask themselves:

> ➢ What do I represent?
> ➢ What is my ideal self?
> ➢ How would I describe myself?
> ➢ What are my values?
> ➢ What is my vision and mission?

Client Value

A sales professional always looks at things through the eyes and perceptions of their clients. They develop a true understanding of what they value. They realize that all clients value different things, as there's no cookie-cutter model available.

The same can be said for different people within the same organization. A sales professional gains an understanding and builds credible relationships with each individual who comprises the buying team. This ensures that their sales conversations are appropriate for each one of them.

> **Sales professionals do not cut corners and assume they know their clients' value.**

By strengthening the relationship, a sales professional gets a better sense of the current business situation and where their clients' desired state is, as this information is used to position their value to address their clients' initiatives, goals, desires, and challenges.

A sales professional will spend as much time as it takes to gain an understanding of their clients' value. They know that taking shortcuts and skimming over key details will result in a failure to create and communicate value.

Company Value

Company values are the guiding principles that are most important to a sales professional about the way a business works, acts, and communicates.

They align their values to the company to create a value-based, go-to-market strategy. They align to the following:

➢ Being accountable
➢ Making a difference
➢ Serving others
➢ Doing what is right

When alignment of values occurs, people understand one another, and everyone does the right things for the right reasons. Value alignment helps the whole company achieve its core mission: taking care of their clients and employees.

When values are out of alignment—with people working towards different goals, and with different intentions and outcomes—this ultimately damages work relationships, productivity, job satisfaction, and creative potential.

How well do you know your company's mission, vision, and value statement?

A sales professional marries values together in harmony, and uses this to take care of their clients as well as to grow new opportunities. This is what I refer to as sales prosperity.

Aligning Value Requires Paying Close Attention

Done with precision, building value positions you with a greater chance to grow sales while building long-term profitable and sustainable business relationships. I encourage you to go back and analyze some of your best client relationships. Grab a sheet of paper and start asking yourself some of the following questions:

> ➢ Do I know what my clients value?
> ➢ Do they know what I value?
> ➢ Do they know what my company values?

If you struggle at any level to answer, then I believe uncovering these issues could be the path to strengthening and insulating your relationships from hostile take-overs.

To take your sales to the next level, I encourage you to pay close attention to the strength of your relationships, tolerance for change, and your clients' current situation. As well, be curious and always ask questions.

It's imperative in today's competitive business environment that sales professionals marry their value, their clients' value, and their company's value together in complete harmony, which is uniquely suited to promote growth and business betterment.

Creating Meaningful Value Starts with Becoming Educated

Whose responsibility is it to ensure that you obtain the skills, knowledge, behavior, and tools needed to engage in meaningful conversations?

Do you know more about what you sell than your clients or future clients? (I would sure hope so!)

Do they believe that you do? Do they see you as an advisor? Are you sharing with them your knowledge of their marketplace? Are you sharing valuable insights and bits of education?

Imagine your clients saying, "Maybe I should listen to this person."

The late great Jim Rohn said,

> *Formal education will make you a living; self-education will make you a fortune.*

Personal accountability and self-education start forming the foundational layers of sales success. How much of your success would you say is up to you? The choices you make, your actions, and your behaviors will make or break you.

If you want to live a prosperous sales life, you must take your own education and learning into your own hands. However, before you start self-educating, you need to convince yourself of the importance of sales success.

Self-Education Starts with Self-Enablement

Self-enablement is about the skills and resources that professionals develop for themselves to insure they rock those business conversations with meaningful value when they gain a seat at the business table.

> **If salespeople cannot articulate their value and their story, or hold a business conversation, then they're dead in the business water.**

Learning is at the core of self-enablement. It's about dedicating the time to increase knowledge about your clients, your future clients, and your industry. It's about developing a new skill or enhancing the tactics you already use. When you do this, you start upping your sales success.

Right now, you might be asking yourself, "Where do I start? How do I become self-enabled?" Self-enablement starts with knowing more than your clients and future clients about your company's products, solutions, or services.

One of your most precious assets are your clients. I encourage you to spend quality time with your clients. No, this doesn't mean the dreaded "stop by to say hello" visit. I mean you should dig in deep, and learn something new about their business, issues, challenges, goals, and initiatives.

You can earn a PhD in business from your clients for free if you are willing to engage with them and learn what is valuable to them.

Sales professionals become students of their clients' businesses; are you doing the same?

Educate Yourself with Meaning

One of the most valuable skills in sales is how to learn. This one skill will help you flourish as your industry evolves. Imagine being forced to explore new opportunities in a rapidly changing work environment. Think about what happens in challenging and uncertain times. What new skill could you learn? What books can you read? What podcasts can you listen to? What new things could you learn specifically from your clients?

You must continually seek opportunities to learn and grow if you want to thrive, survive, and remain valuable to your clients. While that may sound cumbersome and frightening, it is the cold, hard truth.

To stay competitive, you must stay sharp. You must always be learning. The next time the economy shifts, and your company's leadership looks to make cuts, they are going to evaluate which employees have the tenacity and motivation to keep up with their changing needs and which ones have been complacent.

Self-Education: The Key to Value-Based Client Conversations

Let's bring this all back to where we started. Sales professionals have a deep burning desire to learn. It means having a real love for discovery and self-development. It is about being curious and open to learning from failure.

How willing are you to dig in and get messy with learning? You must become responsible for your own education, hold yourself accountable, and do the things to make learning appealing, relevant, useful, and rewarding.

Sales professionals commit to lifelong learning, while sales reps find excuses about why they can't.

> *I want to encourage you never to stop growing.*
> *Become a sales professional who stays at the top of*
> *his/her game by making a commitment to learning*
> *and development.*
> **Larry Levine,** *Selling from the Heart*

Self-education allows you to start living in a way that embodies who you want to become. Think about this and how it applies to your sales career.

➢ Do your clients feel confident in you after they speak with you?
➢ Do your clients believe you are the go-to sales professional in your marketplace?

When was the last time you had a conversation with a client and heard, "Wow, this was one of the best conversations I've ever had!"

When you hear that, then you will know you are on the right track.

Chapter 5 Summary

1. Sales professionals understand that proactive conversations are planned, purposeful, and deliver on their promises.
2. You never know when one conversation will lead to exponential sales growth.
3. Creating value not only transforms sales effectiveness, but it also provides insulation from the price hammer.
4. Sales professionals do not cut corners and assume they know their clients' value.
5. If salespeople cannot articulate their value and their story, or hold a business conversation, then they're dead in the business water.

Chapter 6:

Business Acumen

Don't just get involved. Fight for your seat at the table. Better yet, fight for a seat at the head of the table.
Barack Obama

Meaningful value is the foundation. This is what elevates you inside the business community. Combine this with business acumen and now you are ready to pull up a chair at the business table with executive decision-makers, key influencers, and those who can make a difference.

What is acumen? According to the *Merriam-Webster Dictionary*, it is:

> *A keenness and depth of perception, discernment, or discrimination especially in practical matters. A power to see what is not evident to the average mind.*

Let's focus in on the word "average." You cannot be mediocre or adequate; you must excel beyond what is normal. Average effort gets you average results. Average acumen gets you average conversations. People will remember you if what you do is memorable. Engage in business conversation with high business acumen and there is no way you can be forgotten. Watch what starts to happen next!

Is what you offer distinguishable from what anybody else does? I encourage you to dig in and engage in business conversations that are truly unique. You cannot be average if you want a seat at the business table.

If you wish to gain that coveted seat, you must learn, consume, and mirror their executive business characteristics. All this starts with business acumen.

Don't Expect a Seat if You Don't Bring Anything to the Table

According to Gartner Research,

> *Today's B2B buying involves more stakeholders than ever before. In a typical firm with 100 to 500 employees, an average of seven people are involved in most buying decisions, each armed with four or five pieces of information they have gathered for themselves.*

Regardless of the size of the organization, the market sector, or sales channel you are calling into, your clients are armed with knowledge and insights. What are you doing to marry this with your knowledge and insights to have meaningful value-based conversations? How well are you grabbing the attention of all these decision-makers, and what are you bringing to the business table that is any different?

To reinforce this idea even more, let this quote from Marc Miller, who wrote the book *A Seat at the Table* sink in:

In today's commoditized business world, customers only care about one thing: value. To offer real value, you must stop being a salesperson and become a businessperson who sells.

As we begin this journey to gain a seat at the table, please be radically honest with your answers to the following questions:

➢ Do you have what it takes to gain a seat at the table? If so, why?
➢ Are you bringing business substance to the table? If so, how?

➢ Are you a salesperson or a businessperson who sells?
➢ Are you bringing valuable insights to the conversation? If so, do your clients know it?

These are tough questions, but they're necessary if your goal is to increase your sales.

I ask you to reflect for a moment: What is the difference between a salesperson or a businessperson who sells? The answer is responsibility and accountability.

If you are unwilling to make contributions of significance, then you are a salesperson reeking of commission breath who will never gain the coveted seat at the table.

Equal Business Stature

Consider that each individual sitting at the table has business goals, challenges, dreams, aspirations, and desires. It is up to you to attach your offerings to these various aspects in the form of strategic help to create true value.

At this point, you may be asking yourself, "What is equal business stature?"

I believe that people do business with those they respect, trust, and view as being credible. If you are seen as less capable or less professional, why would someone trust you with their business? Why would your clients continue to do business with you?

First, let's look at what not having equal business stature looks like. This might be the mirror moment you need.

➢ Overly apologetic
➢ Subservient or fearful appearance
➢ Insecure
➢ Ill-prepared
➢ Desperate, and willing to say anything
➢ Unpolished communication

This, my friends, will not lead to the next steps in anyone's business journey.

Perception is reality in the eyes of those who matter. I want you to pause and think about that sentence for a moment. In the Bible, you will see the word "selah". It is a word telling you to stop because what was said was important and you must take it in.

How you appear and how you carry yourself matters. First impressions are everything when it comes to equal business stature.

- ➢ Does your business walk match your business talk?
- ➢ Are you speaking your own sales language, or their business language?
- ➢ How do you perceive yourself?

Projecting and portraying an executive presence, combined with the way you deliver your message, will cause executives and your clients to take notice.

Earn your way to equal business stature by:

- ➢ Being well prepared
- ➢ Being confident
- ➢ Communicating well verbally and in writing
- ➢ Knowing your value
- ➢ Not being intimidated by executives
- ➢ Understanding why you are there, and being willing to walk away if it is not the right fit

This is the holy grail: confidence, competence, business acumen, business conversation, and business knowledge.

Here are a few tips to get you started down the road of gaining equal business stature:

- ➢ Do your due diligence before the first meeting; ask thoughtful, curiosity-filled questions, and offer meaningful contributions.
- ➢ Set the conversation around an outline or agenda, then lead the conversation on agreeable and actionable next steps.
- ➢ Portray a professional image both in person and online.

> ➢ Network, socialize, and build community with other executives; you are judged by your network.
> ➢ Consume knowledge, exercise your vocabulary, and be ready to discuss industry trends and news.
> ➢ Do what you say you will; be honest, authentic, direct, and congruent.

Business Acumen Is Essential for New Business Development

To be a successful sales professional, you must learn to position yourself as a trusted thought leader who delivers insightful education and guidance.

Developing new business is about your ability to create demand for yourself by compelling your clients or future clients to consider a solution to a problem that was never on their agenda or radar screen. This is where business acumen serves you well.

My guilty pleasure is a Grande Americano from Starbucks. As you know, Starbucks is a globally recognized, iconic brand. Starbucks was founded in 1971 by Jerry Baldwin, Zev Siegl, and Gordon Bowker in Seattle, Washington, Pike Place Market.

In the early 1980s, they sold the company to Howard Schultz who fell in love with Starbucks on his first taste. After a visit to Italy in 1983, Schultz was determined to actually brew and sell Starbucks coffee in a European-style coffeehouse. He quickly transformed Starbucks into the nationwide java sensation it has become today.

When Starbucks made this monumental pivot, they did not just go into the coffee-brewing business, they went into the retail industry sector. They went out and started leasing and eventually acquiring commercial real estate property. This was not enough, though. Schultz launched a number of other initiatives to complete this transformation. They had to make investments in a CRM and a loyalty management system to get customers coming back for more.

They also had to implement a supply chain management system to manage the materials from their suppliers. They had to invest in POS (or point of sale systems) that would go inside each Starbucks to process payments.

Eventually, a global network had to be built out for all of those point of sales systems to run seamlessly across the world.

Now, let's stop for a moment and think about this. If you were trying to sell software and/or IT services to Starbucks, but somehow possessed limited business acumen and knowledge, what is the likelihood you would gain Starbucks as a client? Business acumen and business awareness will catapult your sales career.

Referring back to the Starbucks example, please do not feel like you must consume yourself in understanding every detail, but you must understand the following:

➢ How a business assesses their strengths, weaknesses, opportunities, and threats in order to help them determine their current business state.

➢ How they determine their desired future state such as goals, initiatives, dreams, and desires.

➢ How they identify the gaps (if they exist) in order to achieve their desired results.

➢ How they go about developing a strategy to help support hitting their goals.

Sales professionals double-down on the development of business acumen. They see the bigger picture. They understand why it is important and essential.

Their ultimate goal is to have confident business conversations. These types of conversations lead to equal business stature.

The more you focus on this factor, the more genuine your conversations will become. These conversations will become more rewarding as you will be stepping into a true consultative partner position. When you have it, people sense it, and soon turn to you as having a sense for knowing what needs to be done in business situations.

Sales Professionals Consume Business Acumen for Breakfast

Are you communicating clearly with every individual who is sitting at the table and earning their respect? Are you collaborating creatively to help them uncover new ways of doing better business? Are you clearly communicating, collaborating with conciseness, and engaging with your clients to help them do better business?

When digging deeper into business acumen, I came across Ray Reilly, a professor of business administration at the Ross School of Business, University of Michigan. He consults with corporations and has reported how few executives know what business acumen actually is or why it is important.

He describes a person with business acumen as someone who understands the key things they need to know to make a decision, to synthesize complex and apparently unconnected data, and react positively to events when they do not happen as expected. I wholeheartedly believe that this can be applied to sales professionals.

They learn the language of business. They learn the language of business executives, and they speak their language.

You Must Gain an Appetite for Acumen

Remember, C-level executives and mid-level decision-makers are business savvy. You must engage in business-oriented conversations to establish your credibility and to differentiate yourself from the competition.

If you want to establish trust, then speak their language, not yours. You must understand their industry and their competitive environment. Sales professionals understand their clients and future clients' business. Ask yourself the following questions:

- ➢ What are you eating for breakfast?
- ➢ What are you reading and listening to with breakfast?
- ➢ What knowledge do you think business executives consume for breakfast?
- ➢ Where do they get this knowledge?

Sales Professionals Build Their Business Acumen Through Literacy

With daily discipline and determination, sales professionals develop an appetite for business acumen. Increasing your business literacy will improve your business acumen.

I encourage you to:

> ➢ Read company reports.
> ➢ Follow business market trends.
> ➢ Gain a solid understanding of finance.
> ➢ Learn the terminology that businesspeople use.
> ➢ Allow your clients to teach you their business.

One can earn a PhD in business from their clients if they are willing to invest in asking for help.

Sales professionals understand that business literacy is one of the greatest investments they can make. It truly is a gift that keeps on giving. Add business literacy on top of value-based conversations and this becomes rocket fuel for trust-based conversations.

Acumen Is an Asset

The business world is rapidly changing. This does not allow any of you to take your own sweet time to learn new things. You must create acumen urgency if you wish to sit at the head of the business table.

Sales professionals are committed to professional development with the goal of building a disciplined and consistent approach to analyzing business problems, as they use this to help their clients make informed decisions.

To quote my very dear friend, Mike Garrison, author of *Can I Borrow Your Car?*

> *If you only know how to relate based upon what you get paid for, you will only be viewed as an expert on that very subject. On the other hand, if you can demonstrate that you are an expert (or at least a credible peer) on what your prospects get paid for, you are someone that will be welcomed into the 'inner sanctum' of their business and will be a valued and respected advisor . . . no matter what you sell.*

My sales friend's business acumen is an asset and will help you earn the right to sit at the business table.

Great sales professionals dig in with their clients. They peel back the layers with inquisitive and insightful questions. They do not hide behind their products and their company.

As we close this chapter, I would like to share with you a wonderful testimony from Bill McCormick, a dear friend and CEO of Digi-Sales—Where All Selling Is Social:

> *I've always had this internal belief that we can fake things for some time, but eventually, our true selves emerge. This belief for me comes from my faith. Jesus himself said that what is in our hearts will come out of our mouths—whether good or bad.*
>
> *Early in my sales career, I learned many questionable techniques from sales leaders and trainers to "fake it 'til you make it" and this left me with a false sense of what it took to be successful in sales. The focus was on closing the deal or finding the next big deal—always looking to the future and never focused on the client in front of me or the deal that was closed yesterday, or last week, or a few months ago.*
>
> *My heart was always focused on how much value I could provide my client or prospect, and that is what I wanted to focus on. The sales cultures that I was involved in had other ideas. I wished for a better way, but before I could discover that, my life and career took a sharp right turn and I left the sales world.*

In 2021, my wife and I started our own company, and with only a handful of clients, I returned to the world of sales, this time as a co-owner and heading up the sales team—it was a team of three: my, myself, and I. My "team" was determined to not be "salesy" and not fall back on the techniques and strategies I had learned in the past that were based on faking it and getting immediate results, but focused on building long-lasting relationships and partnerships.

I was finally able to focus on providing value to our clients and prospects, and building relationships focused on mutual success for all. I discovered, years later, that I wasn't alone in this approach. I was finally able to sell from my heart, which I came to understand for me was to serve my clients with their best interests at heart.

This is the core message of the Selling from the Heart *movement! In 2020, I was introduced to the book, podcast, and author, Larry Levine. I discovered a community and philosophy that was so congruent with mine that I had to get involved.*

Through participating in several Selling from the Heart *challenges and becoming a part of the insider's group, I have been able to make giant strides in my business, sales, and trust-building acumen.*

I learned the importance of understanding my clients and potential clients' business, their goals (both business and personal), as well as how to engage them in conversation so that we are not just business acquaintances, but we trust each other on a deeper level. This has all made me a better sales professional. If that's all it did for me, it would be huge, but as they say in the infomercial world, "But wait, there's more!"

Selling from the Heart *has also helped me to be a better husband, father, and overall human being.*

When I focus on my heart and what is coming out of my heart through my words and actions, as well as through my fingers in what I type and the messages I send, I am more genuine and people get to know the real me. I've discovered since putting the message into practice that I'm much more focused on serving those around me, both personally and professionally, and when I do that, good things happen. I'm much more focused on helping and serving, not what someone may or may not be able to do for me. My interactions with clients and prospective clients used to be one-sided: What can they do for me? Will they buy from me? Will they give me an introduction to a decision-maker? Now, my interactions with clients and prospects are still one-sided, but to the other end of the spectrum: What can I do for them? What value can I add to their lives? Who can I introduce them to?

Before Selling from the Heart, *I was focused entirely on making a sale and obtaining a customer. After learning the philosophy, I am now much more focused on being curious, uncovering the value I can provide for the person in front of me by being curious, and meeting their needs if I'm able, while still earning what I need financially.*

Chapter 6 Summary

1. Is what you offer distinguishable from what anybody else does? I encourage you to dig in and engage in business conversations that are truly unique. You cannot be average if you want a seat at the business table.

2. If you are unwilling to make contributions of significance, you are a salesperson reeking of commission breath who will never gain the coveted seat at the table.

3. How you appear and how you carry yourself matters. First impressions are everything when it comes to equal business stature.

4. Are you communicating clearly with every individual who is sitting at the table and earning their respect? Are you collaborating creatively to help them uncover new ways of doing better business? Are you clearly communicating, collaborating with conciseness, and engaging with your clients to help them do better business?

5. If you want to establish trust, speak their language, not yours. You must understand their industry and their competitive environment. Sales professionals know their clients and future clients' business.

6. One can earn a PhD in business from their clients if they are willing to invest in asking for help.

Chapter 7:

Traits of a True Sales Professional

Matt sat across the table from the new saleswoman Carly, and he was impressed. Originally, he was not even going to entertain having a meeting with her. He was seriously considering going with a new copier company due to the ineptitude of the salesperson they had been dealing with previously, but Carly was different.

From the first introduction, Carly was curious and genuinely seemed to care about him and his company. It was this encounter that convinced Matt to give her a chance.

As their first official meeting started to unfold, he could tell that she had done her homework. Carly came prepared, understanding his industry. She asked engaging questions and listened carefully, diligently taking notes on Matt's responses. She got to know him personally and they realized that they both had a love of the Scouting movement and how it allowed both boys and girls to live up to their potential.

As the meeting concluded, Carly promised to get back to Matt regarding a few points she needed to confirm and promised to have the answers back to him within a day—which she did. Matt decided he would stay with the company, and over the years, a great professional relationship developed between them that they both benefitted greatly from.

Success Leaves Clues

Mediocre, average, ordinary, or complacent: these would not be qualities associated with successful salespeople. Curiosity, on the other hand, is one of the key qualities of a sales professional.

Curious professionals make an impact, achieve success, and smash their sales targets. Being insanely curious is a required character trait if you wish to master business disruptions and bring meaningful value to your clients. All sales professionals put their learning into overdrive; do you?

A naturally curious professional places themselves in their client's shoes, digs in deep to uncover business barriers, and then guides them down the road to business betterment.

Walt Disney once said,

> *When you are curious, you find lots of interesting things to do.*

What is your daily appetite for curiosity?

Curiosity is an essential part of discovering how to bring meaningful value. It drives your ability to make new connections and engage. The more engaged you become, the more inclined you are to ask meaningful questions. The more you learn and uncover, the more you grow the relationship.

I believe a curious professional:

➢ Is enthusiastic and takes interest in their career.
➢ Is open-minded.
➢ Is inquisitive and wants to know why.
➢ Is not shy to ask questions and seek out answers.

If you're not a naturally curious person, that's okay. Curiosity can be developed with the right mindset.

When I think about curious salespeople, the phrases and words that come to mind are: intense desire to know something, eagerness, questioning, interested, detectives, thirst for knowledge, and inquisitive.

Taking it up one additional level, insanely curious salespeople are constantly thirsty for success!

> **Curiosity is mission-critical to your sales success as it signals a hungry mind.**

Being inquisitive means you are open to new experiences. It is through these new experiences that you can generate more original ideas, leading to simple solutions to complex problems for your clients. This, my friend, is value nirvana.

Curious Sales Professionals Smash Their Sales Targets

Being curious means always wondering *why*. Curious salespeople think and act on a different plane. They identify and ask questions, soliciting deeper results. Sales reps ask surface-level questions, whereas sales professionals dig below the surface to uncover the root cause.

Sales Professionals Value Curiosity

According to the *Oxford English Dictionary*, curiosity is a strong desire to know or learn something. Truly curious people are not afraid to try, explore, and question things, and then turn them inside out.

I truly believe it is more effective to act as if no one knows you or recognizes the value you bring, as this makes you have to prove it every day. Are you proving your value daily to your clients? What does it look like? Can you define it? Do your clients know that you are bringing value? If so, when was the last time you discussed this with them?

Curious salespeople have no issues asking their clients the following:

➢ What value do my services, products, or solutions create for you?
➢ What does value-added look like to you?
➢ How would you describe meaningful value? And when was the last time you experienced it?

Sustaining value in the minds of your clients requires persistence and extreme focus. This is what curious salespeople are all about: an obsession with understanding value.

Curious Professionals Take Responsibility

Average sales reps make excuses and point fingers for everything bad that happens to them: It's the economy; the leads are weak; the competition has better products; buyers are idiots; we are too expensive; our service is horrible. My advice to you is to stop the freaking excuses!

Curious salespeople see these challenges as learning opportunities. They learn to do something different and practice different ways of progressing towards achieving sales success. They become obsessed with identifying as many ways as possible to improve. They are open-minded to finding novel ways of enhancing their sales career.

Sales Professionals Are Curious About Their Clients

Top sales professionals know their clients deserve more than just a "check-in" or "touching base" phone call. They recognize the importance of exploring their clients' beliefs, challenges, motivations, and, most essentially, what they want to accomplish.

> **Innately curious salespeople are ready to ask the right questions, provide the right insights, and respond with answers. This, my friend, is value.**

I am curious,

- ➤ Are you making sure your clients feel special before, during, and after doing business with you?
- ➤ Are you making your clients feel important?
- ➤ Do your clients feel that you care about them?
- ➤ Do your clients feel like they can trust you?

Curious salespeople focus on developing conversations, not sales campaigns. It is about opening up human-to-human conversation.

> ## When was the last time you had a conversation with one of your clients that did not involve trying to sell them something?

If you have, what did you learn? How did your clients feel about this conversation? If you have not, I ask you to think about all the learning moments and what you can uncover about them.

What would it look like for you if you became more curious on behalf of your clients? What could you help your clients do better? With curious intent, spend time with your clients and ask them how you have been enhancing their experience.

> ## Stop and think for a moment . . .

The one thing separating successful salespeople from all the others who are merely surviving or, should I say, comfortably complacent, is their desire to learn.

Successful salespeople never stop learning. In turn, they translate their new understandings into innovative ideas for their clients. I encourage you to break out of the complacent, default modes of thinking. Recycling old ideas with traditional sales approaches does not help you smash your targets or satisfy your clients.

> ## Success breeds complacency.

Operate within your sales career based upon curiosity and watch what happens to perceived value. Is this not what you want?

Curiosity Leads to Connection and It Starts at the Heart

> *The best and most beautiful things in the world*
> *cannot be seen or even touched—*
> *they must be felt with the heart.*
> **Helen Keller**

Your ability to succeed becomes crippled when there's an unbalanced connection with your heart. Embracing a heart-centered approach to sales rests with your ability to pause, look inward, and reflect upon the course of action you know is the right one, rather than succumbing to external pressures and misaligned sales tactics.

Sales professionals who unify at the heart level (as opposed to the wallet level) are able to connect with the emotional needs of their clients. They understand people crave the need to be valued, respected, seen, heard, and acknowledged.

By acknowledging the human element, heart-centered professionals maintain the wisdom to positively transform their clients' business experience.

Heart and Kindness

According to relationship expert John Gottman, if you want connectivity, mutual affinity, care, passion, trust, longevity, and respect, then you must choose to be kind. Consider the following questions:

➢ Are you going the extra mile with your clients?
➢ Are you honoring and delighting them when they least expect it?
➢ How are you building trust with your clients?
➢ Are you a valuable member of their team?

Zappos, Nordstrom, and Starbucks have all benefited financially from their loyal customers. A few years back, Starbucks launched their kindness campaign. Nordstrom and Zappos continue to wow customers with their generous return policies.

At what level are you connecting with your clients?

> ## A *Selling from the Heart* sales professional seeks first to understand, as they turn transactional sales opportunities into transformational experiences.

One of the kindest things you can do for your clients is to listen to them. I am referring to the type of listening that shows genuine interest and authentic care.

When you listen at this level, you are giving your full presence and attention. It is about connecting and relating. This happens through intentionally listening. This is one valuable gift you can give to your clients.

Connecting With Heart Is Not a Sign of Weakness

Honoring and connecting with your heart is not a sign of weakness. True power resides with listening to your "gut" and finding it within your heart by making a commitment to clear all that stands in the way of a heartfelt connection.

I encourage you to remove the self-induced boundaries within your mind that say, "I can't go there" or "I'm not sure." Go there and watch what happens when you remove the barrier to the heart.

Sharing your knowledge is not a sign of weakness. Focus on how you can help. Sharing is caring. Share your insights and what you can do for others rather than for yourself. I guarantee that no one likes a know-it-all, self-centered, and stereo-typical sales rep. This does not build followership, nor is it valued.

Sales professionals wake up every day with a learn-it-all mindset; sales reps wake up with a know-it-all mindset. A *Selling from the Heart* professional focuses on the concept of connecting with honesty and integrity. They walk, talk, live, and breathe the human aspect of sales. They lead a congruent lifestyle.

They are true practitioners and minister to their clients the message of *Selling from the Heart*. They measure their success not by their commission check, but on the impact they have made on their clients.

A Heartfelt Sales Professional

I believe that sales professionals must:

> ➢ Make themselves available to serve.
> ➢ Pay attention to their clients.
> ➢ Complete every task with equal dedication.
> ➢ Become faithful and trustworthy.
> ➢ Care about their career, their clients, and their livelihood.

A *Selling from the Heart* professional values themselves. What are your values?

True sales professionals connect deeply to the idea of serving others. They are humble, genuine, and sincere as they roll up their emotional sleeves. Loving and deeply connecting with their clients while delivering results is their two-headed sales coin.

Heart and Value

To build meaningful value, you must know what it truly is. Why is this so important? Inside a sea of sales sameness, *value* irrefutably becomes one of the single biggest connection factors. A true professional recognizes the value in both their sales-based tools and their heart-based tools. They are skillful in building rock-solid and credible relationships.

They display kindness and concern. They understand that these emotions demonstrate strength rather than weakness.

Heartfelt professionals are not afraid to use the most powerful tools that come from the heart. Be different, think different, and act different. It is imperative to marry your value, your client's value, and your company's value in complete harmony in order to promote growth and better business.

Are You a Heartfelt Sales Professional?

A *Selling from the Heart* professional deeply touches the hearts and minds of their clients. This becomes invaluable and irreplaceable. If these traits resonate with you, then you are on the path towards becoming a heartfelt sales professional.

> ➤ You are committed to personal and professional growth.
> ➤ You have compassion for yourself and others.
> ➤ You have the willingness to look in the mirror and come to terms with your own character flaws.
> ➤ You're committed to making a difference not only in your own life, but in the lives of your clients.
> ➤ You simply care.

I urge you all of you to lead a sales life full of authenticity and integrity rather than the pursuit of lining your sales wallet.

The Value of a Giving Lifestyle

According to Wharton Professor Adam Grant in his book *Give and Take*, there are three types of people in the world when it comes to reciprocity styles: givers, takers, and matchers.

> *In a world where we often work in teams and provide services to others, we should strive to adopt a giver mentality. Givers are more successful because they establish reputations and relationships that enhance their success over the long term.*

Can a giving mindset in a sales world riddled with unscrupulous, fake, and disingenuous people be the answer? A giver is always trying to figure out what they can do for others. "How can I be of help? How may I be of value?" A taker is always trying to figure out how to gain something from the situation.

Is giving the secret to long-term sales success?

Ask a group of salespeople why they got into sales, and you will hear many say, "For the money." Making money is not evil, nor is being wealthy. The evil happens when you place your commissions before people and their visions.

The Value of a Giving Mindset

Are you giving without asking for anything in return? I have become fascinated by the Japanese philosophy of Omotenashi. This can simply be translated as hospitality.

In the West, we tend to see hospitality as providing exceptional customer service with the expectation to receive something in return. In Japanese culture, it is providing exceptional customer service without the assumption of receiving a reward. *The Michelin Guide* breaks down the meaning of the Japanese word:

> *"Omote" means public face—an image you wish to present to outsiders. "Nashi" means nothing. Combining them means every service is from the bottom of the heart—honest, no hiding, no pretending.*

A *Selling from the Heart* professional is all about giving and serving. They integrate Omotenashi in creating the most heartfelt client experiences. What's inside your heart that, in turn, you can give to your clients?

**The more you give of yourself,
the more you find yourself.**

The Value of Giving from the Heart

Giving of your heart is not a sign of weakness; it is true strength. To give without expecting anything back shows that you do not need others to fulfil the emotional, mental, or physical needs in your life. Real power resides with listening to your inner voice by making a commitment to clear all that stands in the way of a heartfelt connection.

A *Selling from the Heart* professional aligns themselves in the direction of their clients, looking at giving more than they receive. They are completely focused on helping.

> ## Heartfelt professionals focus on making a real difference while having a positive impact on others.

I encourage you to integrate Omotenashi with your clients by doing the following:

- ➢ Anticipate their needs
- ➢ Be selfless
- ➢ Be considerate

Givers Establish Human Engagement

Heartfelt givers establish reputations and strong relationships, enhancing their success over the long term. Their human approach to relationships builds trust, encourages open conversation, and creates value for their clients rather than simply claiming value.

A giving approach may not be fruitful in the short term, but it is incredibly valuable and powerful in the long run.

Givers engage through heartfelt questions. The end result is that their clients feel respected and valued, feeling more comfortable in sharing information. By asking engaging questions, givers are learning what their clients value.

Adam Grant states in his book, *Give and Take*,

> *By asking questions and getting to know their customers, givers build trust and gain knowledge about their customers' needs. Over time, this makes them better and better at selling.*

Think about the following:

> ## What would happen to your client relationships if you asked great questions, created a giving

mindset, and integrated the Japanese philosophy of Omotenashi?

Imagine knowing your clients so well that you anticipate their needs before they do. Omotenashi is a *Selling from the Heart* professional. Are you that person?

The Servant's Heart Is Invaluable

Being a servant-led professional means putting the interests of others above your own. Do you put others before yourself? If you are afraid to do this, then why is that? Have you given thought as to what this may be costing you? If not, then think about it.

If you are afraid to be vulnerable, ditch that fear. Remove the mask; just rip it off! Vulnerability is one of the greatest traits you can embrace.

Embracing our vulnerabilities is risky, but not nearly as dangerous as giving up on love and belonging and joy—the experiences that make us the most vulnerable. Only when we are brave enough to explore the darkness will we discover the infinite power of our light.
Brené Brown

Old-school bravado and a bragging mindset no longer work in today's sales climate. No one cares what you have accomplished in your sales career. They want to know how much you care about them.

To me, the art of serving is not manipulative, deceitful, or disingenuous. It is genuinely caring about somebody and their company. In your heart of hearts, you are there to help them do better business.

Caring is deeply rooted in the servant mindset. Apply caring to your clients and watch what happens to your relationships, the interactions, and the outcomes. It is fine to not care about what does not matter as long as you do care about what does. One of the best ways to ensure clients feel valued and appreciated is to serve them up the gift of caring.

Caring is not hard. It's saying, "I'll be here for you at all times. I have your best interest at heart." Deeply invest and authentically care about the experiences your clients have with you, and then watch your results skyrocket.

> *The servant-leader is servant first. . . . It begins with the natural feeling that one wants to serve, to serve first. Then conscious choice brings one to aspire to lead.*
> **Robert Greenleaf**

The greatest gift a servant professional can give is themselves. Give of yourself without expecting anything in return. This is irrefutable value. I must ask, how well are you serving others, and what is your guide?

Serve Up the Inner Circle

Someone who is authentic, willing to lead, and is there to help their clients do better business brings in their inner circle—their centers of influence. They connect them with the other clients they know that can help them do even better business. This is truly serving with the heart.

> *It is one of the most beautiful compensations of life that no man can sincerely try to help another without helping himself . . . Serve and thou shall be served.*
> **Ralph Waldo Emerson**

When you serve with the heart, it will always come back to you, whether in sales, referrals, or personal and business recommendations. When you do good, people notice. Conversely, they also notice when you don't, and trust me, they can be very vocal about it.

Win the Value War: Serve with Your Heart

In a business world where those in sales are viewed with negativity, an authentic, real-deal approach is a breath of fresh air. It may result in losing a few battles, but those who put their hearts and clients first are guaranteed to win the war.

➢ A servant sales professional has an authentic desire to serve.
➢ A servant sales professional is all in.
➢ A servant sales professional is focused on serving the needs of the person sitting in front of them.

Whoever wants to become a valued sales professional must become a servant!

Have you viewed the Trust Formula Mini-Course at www.sellinginaposttrustworld.com yet? This is a valuable free course to help you on your journey to becoming a true sales professional.

Chapter 7 Summary

1. Curiosity is mission-critical to your sales success as it signals a hungry mind.
2. Being curious means always wondering why. Curious salespeople think and act on a different plane. They identify and ask questions that solicit deeper results.
3. Innately curious salespeople are ready to ask the right questions, provide the right insight, and respond with answers. This is true value.
4. When was the last time you had a conversation with one of your clients that did not involve trying to sell them something?
5. A *Selling from the Heart sales professional seeks first to understand as they turn transactional sales opportunities into transformational experiences.*
6. What would happen to your client relationships if you asked great questions, created a giving mindset, and integrated the Japanese philosophy of Omotenashi?

Section 3:

Inspirational Experiences

Our lives are shaped through experiences. Memories, pleasant and unpleasant, have permanently left a mark and altered our outlook on everything. Our experiences influence our reasoning, perceptions, ideas, beliefs, and judgment.

Stop and think for a moment: how are the experiences you are providing your clients affecting their perception of you? Would you even know?

Experiences and feelings often lie dormant for a long time, only to rise to the surface the minute we encounter a similar circumstance. Unfortunately, with trust and credibility at an all-time low, it's time to assess the experiences you are providing to your clients. How are these experiences determining what happens next? Can you be sealing your fate without being aware of it?

If you are conscious of how important personal experiences are to you and how these influence your life, then I encourage you to draw upon the significance of these experiences to recreate them for your clients.

At some point, you may have become the victim of your experiences. However, you can change your thinking by altering the negative memories through creating new and positive ones. Now, how can you apply this thinking to your clients' reasoning when it comes to their past experiences with salespeople?

Do you believe in your heart that you can influence opinions? I believe that you can. We all have the capability of influencing opinions, thoughts, understanding, memories, feelings, and responses by how we choose to behave.

By making a conscious effort to create a positive encounter and experience every time you interact with one of your clients, you have immediately started to create pleasant memories, experiences, and contentment. Once established, think about how easy it will be to seek out referrals.

Successful coaches, leaders, and motivators are all experience-makers. They motivate and inspire through positive experiences, lessons, and stories. They inject positivity to move us in ways that we feel we could not do ourselves.

How exhilarating would it be to bring positivity, good deeds and experiences to your clients? I ask you to draw upon the courage, strength, and inner fortitude to bring inspiration to your clients. This will forever change the relational course, and take you on journeys you never would have imagined.

I believe that you have the internal power to inspire your clients and, for that matter, everyone you meet with positive experiences. It's your choice. Perception is reality. At this moment, think about the kind of experiences you are creating for your clients. How would your clients describe them? What words would they use? What are they telling others?

You are in control of the experiences you provide to your clients.

Do not waste the opportunity to positively capture your client experiences. Can inspirational experiences become the missing link to meaningful action with your clients?

Read this partial poem, titled "Don't Just," by Roy T. Bennett from his book, *The Light in the Heart*, and key in on the last word of every sentence.

Don't just learn, experience.
Don't just read, absorb.
Don't just change, transform.
Don't just relate, advocate.
Don't just promise, prove.
Don't just criticize, encourage.

As we go through the chapters in this section, I ask you to reflect upon the last word of every sentence, focus in on each of them to create inspirational experiences for your clients.

Chapter 8:

Your Client's Feelings Matter

Leadership is about making others better
as a result of your presence and making sure
that impact lasts in your absence.
Sheryl Sandberg

L
eaders inspire and influence others to see and achieve things they
believe they couldn't do on their own.

The ability to inspire is one key leadership skill distinguishing
great leaders from average ones. There are plenty of exceptional bosses
out there, but there are only a handful of leaders who are able to infuse
energy, passion, purpose, and connection into their actions and behaviors.

These leaders have a clear vision, mission, and commitment to
integrity. This guides them in everything they do to make the world a
better place.

I believe these characteristics can be applied to a *Selling from the
Heart* professional. Sales professionals are indeed leaders. They inspire
their clients into business betterment through heartfelt experiences.

Inspiration, combined with memorable experiences, becomes the
catalyst, the jet fuel, for deep client loyalty and long-term sustainable
relationships. The consummate professional helps their clients paint a

picture of what could be, as together they cast vision and work towards painting a brighter future.

Speaking of heart, I love this quote, courtesy of Pastor Craig Groeschel:

We do not need a title to lead. We just need to care. People would rather follow a leader with heart than a leader with a title.

Applied to sales, your clients and future clients would rather follow a sales professional who cares and leads with heart as opposed to a sales rep who is an empty suit.

How Are You Making Your Clients Feel?

The feeling is often the deeper truth, the opinion the more superficial one.
Augustus William Hare

Think about this quote for a moment: "The feeling is often the deeper truth." How are you making your clients feel, and could the way they feel be their truth about you?

Philosopher William James was one of the leading thinkers of the late nineteenth century. He was one of the most influential philosophers in the United States, and the father of American psychology.

He once wrote,

The deepest principle in human nature is the craving to be appreciated.

Appreciation makes us feel valued and revered. Being appreciated is how you recognize you are important to others and that your presence makes a difference in someone's life.

Now, think about your clients and your interactions with them. Do your clients feel valued and revered in your presence?

This can be further reinforced through Victor Frankl, who was a psychiatrist and Holocaust survivor. His approach to psychotherapy was called *logotherapy*. This is a therapeutic approach that helps people find personal meaning in life. He said,

> *Meaning gives us purpose and purpose presents us with the endurance to carry onward through difficult times.*

What can we learn from these great thinkers of the past? While *meaning* motivates us, *appreciation* transcends us.

When was the last time you shared with your clients how much you appreciate them?

Think about the competitive sales landscape, and now reflect upon your clients for a moment. How you make them feel could be the key that unlocks the door to monumental sales growth.

Feelings Are Based on Experiences

Are you creating business betterment, or are you more worried about pushing products and services?

Your clients and how you make them feel are the key to your success. They are no longer at the mercy of you, your team, or your company. They have a plethora of options. In fact, many are more interested in the experience you provide them, as opposed to your products or services. You must be able to adapt to their ever-changing needs.

Client experience goes beyond service. It is about how are you making them feel.

I would like for you to pause and think about the following:

In a few words, how would your clients best describe the experience they are receiving from you? And, yes, you can control this.

> ➤ Are you personalizing the level of service?
> ➤ Are you in consistent contact?
> ➤ Are you listening to your clients?

If you are struggling to answer these questions, then I imagine these will be difficult as well:

How well are you creating positive experiences, memories, and feelings?

> ➤ Are you committed?
> ➤ Are you willing to do what is necessary?

If the answer is yes, then you have taken the first step towards client betterment.

Feelings Do Matter!

Maya Angelou famously said:

I've learned that people will forget what you said, people will forget what you did, but people will never forget how you made them feel.

Don Barden in his book, *The Perfect Plan,* shares,

The average person remembers only 6% of a presentation just 10 minutes after it is done.

Stew on that one for a moment, as Don continues on to say,

People make decisions based on the sum of facts and emotions. These emotions make up 85% of the decision, and they are justified with 15% of the facts. Yet, within 10 minutes after the decision or presentation, a person can recall only

6% of the facts, but they recall 100% of how they felt when they experienced the facts.

Again, I will ask you to think, as your clients' feelings and how you are making them feel about you could become the match that lights your long-term sales sustainability.

Your Client Relationships

Ralph Waldo Emerson once said:

To be yourself in a world that is constantly trying to make you something else is the greatest accomplishment.

Be yourself. Your clients deserve the best version of you, not a facade and not a sales pretender, but a true sales professional.

Deep client relationships turn into long-term, consistent, and profitable business.

Can you honestly answer the following?

➤ Do you *really understand what your clients want?*
➤ Are you even relevant in their eyes?
➤ How are you making them feel when you see, speak, or interact with them?

Now, I would like for you to think about one of your largest clients, and how much they mean to you and your company.

What would it mean to you if they took their business elsewhere? How would you feel?

Your clients are the single most important factor towards your long-term success. Therefore, the more successful you become in understanding and forming meaningful relationships with your clients, the more successful you will become.

In a world where trust is literally at rock bottom, no wonder many (including some of your clients) are skeptical about what salespeople say, how they say it, why they say it, and how this makes them feel.

Selling from the Heart Case Study: Kevin Hambrice, CEO TerraSource

Applying what I have learned from Larry Levine and Selling from the Heart *has transformed the way our organization views and approaches relationships—from our employees, suppliers, selling partners, end users, and within our own community. In his book* Selling from the Heart, *Larry articulates how reflecting on and understanding the significance of your individual makeup and true authenticity can bring about new levels of impact with your customers (internal and external). This open and transparent collaboration drives honest communication in new and productive ways. He further reveals how social media and networks can allow connections and learning like never before, which he shows will reinforce the relationship!*

I got to know Larry through a common colleague that suggested I reach out and learn more. We connected virtually, then began a series of video chats and developed a relationship around some of the needs of our sales team. Larry carries out his own business relationships just like his book says. His walk follows his talk!

Larry led our team on an eight-week deep-dive read through his book, and challenged our executive and commercial team to think, put a plan together, and act. Each week was dedicated to a high-level review of the chapter and, most importantly, apply committed examples and learnings the following week in the field. This allowed our team to see immediate results, and then check and adjust our planning efforts.

We found that while techniques come and go, the real element of work that created a sustaining effect was putting more focus on the relationship. This led to more meaningful conversations that then led to opportunities to develop our business solutions. We also found that we needed to develop more specific and individual relationships with long-time customer accounts to strengthen those connections, which were way too fragile and had too many blind spots. This exercise also drove home our need to dial in our value proposition, one that was consistent, so that we shared a common message.

Following our deep-dive book read, Larry came and visited our team (as part of our annual sales meeting) and lead some face-to-face training and coaching modules that reinforced our previous learning as well as role playing to help our team take it to the next level. He spent time with each of our members, getting to know them and to understand where they each were coming from. He helped us validate each of our action plans.

I can say without a doubt that his book is an inspiration to anyone taking a business through a transformational journey. This book has helped me connect with current and new relationships with clearer focus and expectations. It has also become a guide to be a better coach for the organization I have the privilege of working with. With deeper and meaningful relationships, you can have higher expectations, which will deliver results you have never seen before!

Stop Allowing Yourself to Grow Your Competitor's Next Great Client

How do you truly know that you are delivering value to your clients? Are you really giving them what they value more effectively than your competitors? How sure are you?

It is not a good idea to take your clients' loyalty for granted. Meeting their expectations is just not good enough. Your clients want to know that you care. I truly believe that it is more effective to act as if no one knows you or recognizes the value you bring because this will make you show it every day.

Would you know the last time you met with one of your clients and asked them, *"What value do my services, products, or solutions create for you?"* Hopefully, your answer is not "It's been a while" or "Never."

I encourage you to think about this question: *"What does value added look like to your clients?"* I bet your clients want to increase sales and grow their client base, correct?

If so, here is an exercise for you. Write down these two questions, then take some quiet time, relax, and answer them:

> ➢ How do I help my clients gain a competitive advantage?
> ➢ What is my client's perception of value when working with me?

Stay Top of Mind, or Become an Afterthought

Sustaining meaningful value in the minds of your clients requires persistence, extreme focus, and inspirational experiences.

Think about the following and then think about your clients:

> ➢ What is happening right now within their business?
> ➢ What changes (if any) may be happening to them right now?
> ➢ What problems may they be facing?
> ➢ What difficulties are they encountering in their marketplace?

If you are not spending quality time in getting to know your clients better, then I guarantee that someone else will be. Creating true, authentic, and genuine relationships requires spending informal time with your clients.

Do you *really* know what is important to your clients and their business? I believe true leadership for a sales professional is their ability to affect change and to become influential inside their current accounts. With all sincerity, when salespeople get to know their clients inside and out, they can then start to personalize the attention they give to them.

Start Treating Customers as Clients

As we close this chapter, ask yourself: Do you view your customers as customers, or do you view them as clients? How many refer to themselves as clients, but who you treat as customers?

How do you know when a customer becomes a client, or the other way around? When a client becomes a customer, this becomes a problem.

Simply put, customers buy things; clients seek advice.

> ### Are you building customers, or are you building clients?

You cannot expect to get Nordstrom's level of service at Target or Walmart!

Think long and hard about this one. Are you being viewed as a sales rep who sells products and services, or are you viewed as someone who enlightens, adds value, informs, advises, nurtures, and becomes an advocate on behalf of their clients?

Do you prefer to be sold or served? When you are in the marketplace as a consumer, do you seek out professionals whom you can trust, or sleaze-balls selling you and then moving on?

As a true professional, you must hold yourself accountable to build meaningful relationships with your clients who value your expert advice rather than banging on them to make a one-time purchase. An ever-flowing relationship funnel will fuel an ever-flowing sales funnel.

If you fail to keep your clients as such, they could turn into customers. In today's complex business environment, it is the ideas, insight, information, help, and guidance you provide that will continually earn you the privilege of doing business with your clients.

I encourage you to initiate conversations focused on their future needs, upcoming projects, and areas of potential growth. I will leave you to think about this question:

Are you growing your competitor's next great client?

Chapter 8 Summary

1. I believe these characteristics can be applied to a *Selling from the Heart professional. Sales professionals are leaders. They inspire their clients into business betterment through heartfelt experiences.*
2. *Appreciation makes us feel valued and revered. Being appreciated is how you recognize that you are important to others, and that your presence makes a difference in someone's life.*
3. Are you creating business betterment, or are you more worried about pushing products and services?
4. Deep client relationships turn into long-term, consistent, and profitable business.
5. Sustaining meaningful value in the minds of your clients requires persistence, extreme focus, and inspirational experiences.
6. Are you building customers or clients?

Chapter 9:

Are You Boring Your Clients?

Boring salespeople sell products.
Sales professionals sell an inspirational experience.
Larry Levine

enry set his cell phone down in disbelief. He then proceeded to stare off into the sunset while sitting at his desk. "How could this $%$%!% happen?" he thought to himself, "Not them. They've been with us for an eternity. How am I going to break the news to my manager?" He decided to muster up enough courage and went for it. "I might as well get this over with . . ." he thought.

The conversation went better than expected; Henry's boss was disappointed, but not surprised. Unfortunately, this had been a common occurrence over the past several months. They deeply discussed what they could do about it to avoid this happening again. Henry suggested they should call the client and conduct an exit interview, if they were willing. The manager thought it was a fantastic idea. Henry then spoke to his contact at the company, and Pete agreed to meet.

The conversation was an eye-opener for Henry. He soon realized that for quite some time, he had been ignoring them, lulling himself into a state of complacency. He could not remember the last time he had spoken to Pete, or when he had done anything to express his gratitude for their business.

When Henry shared what he unpacked with his manager, they immediately put a plan of action together. This was to ensure that all clients were kept in contact with, felt appreciated, and heard. Guess what? Their clients not only stayed with them, but recommended them to other businesses.

I am reminded of this quote from James Allen: "No duty is more urgent than that of returning thanks." Gratitude and passion are the two main traits of sales professionals who sell inspirational experiences.

How likely will your clients continue to do business with you or get inspired by you if you fail to appreciate and genuinely thank them for their business? Being grateful is a monumental first step in forming a meaningful relationship, providing confidence, and building true loyalty with your clients.

You must have passion in order to inspire. If you are not passionate about what you do, how you do it, and why you do it, then it soon becomes challenging to inspire others into action. To inspire others, you must be able to not only bring forth emotion in yourself, but in your clients. Passion in inspirational leaders is contagious, especially when you see them get excited about and living out their beliefs. Passion not only inspires, but also motivates others into action.

Boredom is the root of all evil—the despairing refusal to be oneself.
Soren Kierkegaard

The root of all evil for many in sales is an empty pipeline. However, I am here to inform you that there is one more evil: boredom. Stop for a brief moment and reflect upon the experience you are providing to your clients.

Can you describe the experience? Can your clients describe the experience? What words would they use to describe the experience?

What has happened to raising the bar, going above and beyond, and creating an "icing-on-the-cake, cherry-on-top" sales experience?

Dictionary.com defines "boring" as:

> ➢ Causing or marked by boredom; dull and uninteresting; tiresome.
> ➢ A boring discussion; to have a boring time.

When you think about your clients, what types of discussions are you having with them? What types of experiences are you creating for them? How would they describe your conversations with them? Are you exciting your clients into business betterment? Or, are you boring your clients, lulling them into business complacency?

B2B means business to business, not boring and too bland.

Your sales life should be lived by the old Boy Scout motto, "Be Prepared," meaning you are to take care of your clients better than anyone else can or will. Let's face it, your clients have choices and they do interact with other salespeople. Are you imparting upon them your knowledge to help them into business betterment? Are you ensuring they are well taken care of?

What concerns me is why the sales world continues to swim in the red ocean. On one side of the coast, I call this the Ocean of Mediocrity, and on the other side, I call this the Ocean of Indistinguishability. Instead, learn how to swim in the deep blue Ocean of Sales Professionalism where there is trust, loyalty, and consistently repeated business.

Stop Making Them Yawn!

Right now, I ask you, are you making your clients yawn? What's even worse, how many of your clients are ignoring or possibly even *ghosting* you? Would you even know?

Believe me or not, being boring is a choice. Many of you have been whimsically lulling your clients into a sense of boredom. For some, they have been doing business with you for so long that they have become numb to your services, and they have settled for boring.

"All of sudden," like a streak of lightening, you are taken aback as a shiny new sales professional comes along, listens to them, and delivers an "icing-on-the-cake" experience, helping them realize they have better options. Keep in mind the following:

> Boring salespeople sell products. Sales professionals sell inspirational experiences.

> Boring salespeople believe they really know their clients. Sales professionals dig in and learn as much as they can about their clients.

> Boring salespeople have nothing new to add to their clients because their talk is product-centric. Sales professionals consistently provide new ideas, novel insights, and continually strive to help their clients do better business.

> Boring salespeople talk at their clients as they broadcast sales jargon. Sales professionals engage in open, honest, and genuine conversations with their clients. They listen, keep them informed, and adapt to their feedback.

> Boring salespeople fail to learn new things about their clients. They struggle to look to the future. They do not learn about their clients and where their business is heading. Sales professionals deeply understand what motivates their clients so they can meet their needs in the future, instead of just in the present moment.

If you are not careful and client-centric, it is easy to fall into habits that deliver client disinterest. On the other hand, innovative, insightful, and inspirational sales professionals breathe life into their client relationships as they dedicate themselves to newness. It is this commitment that keeps their clients coming back for more and referring them often to others.

What Boring Salespeople Do

Boring salespeople focus their attention on simply generating the next sale. On the flip side, a sales professional focuses on building long-term client relationships.

A transactional mindset and product-centric behaviors can be felt by your clients. If this is how you are behaving, I promise that you will be replaced by a better transactional conversation.

Boring and transactional-oriented salespeople provide no reason for their clients to remain loyal. Why should they?

Boredom is only for boring people with no imagination.
Tim Tharp

Do not be that boring salesperson without imagination; instead, be someone your clients anticipate interacting with.

Boring Salespeople Lack Vision

Uninspiring salespeople lack vision, clarity, and breathe no value into their lifeless relationships.

Sales professionals have an inspiring vision fueled by emotion. This vision lights a fire within their clients igniting passion, creativity, and collaboration all towards business betterment.

A consummate sales professional continually evaluates themselves to improve their results and to become better at what they do. Boring salespeople struggle to clearly define themselves and their vision. If you are struggling with clearly seeing and casting your vision, then it will become difficult to help your clients navigate to business prosperity.

Boring Sales Reps Are Not Relevant

Boring salespeople wrap themselves up with self-delusional thoughts regarding how much their clients love them. Furthermore, the relationships that many in sales believe they have with their clients are not nearly what their clients believe them to be.

To become relevant, you need to understand their wants, needs, tensions, desires, and aspirations. Uncovering all of this takes work, dedication, and massive action.

In today's sales world, relevancy is not an option.

Boring salespeople lack relevance because they fail to understand what is meaningful to their clients. Sales professionals discover the emotional and human motivators by taking a genuine interest in their clients' lives.

It's time for some self-reflection. Grab a sheet of paper and a pen, and answer the following questions:

> ➢ Am I going the extra distance for my clients? Now describe it.
> ➢ Am I serving my clients proactively? Now describe it.
> ➢ Am I developing a deep, genuine concern for my clients? Now describe it.
> ➢ Am I looking out for my client's best business interest? Now describe it.

If you can answer yes to these questions, and can truthfully describe your responses, then you are on the right track. If the answer is no, then you have some work to do.

Squash Boredom: Educate, Engage, and Excite

In an environment that is becoming increasingly competitive, you must focus on building meaningful relationships with your clients.

Let's face reality; your clients have choices. Therefore,

> ➢ You must become genuinely interested in their business.
> ➢ You must be on the lookout to help them do better business.
> ➢ You must connect with meaning, rather than contacting them to sell a product or waiting for them to contact you.

What are you doing to engage and build community with your clients?

Allow this quote to sink in:

Bore, N. A person who talks
when you wish him to listen.
Ambrose Bierce

Are you listening to your clients, or talking to your clients?

As we close out this chapter, I want to share with you a case study from Ben St. Clair, Senior Learning Designer, MarketPoint Retail Sales Learning & Development for Humana, on the difference that *Selling from the Heart* has made in his company.

> *"I want to read this book!"*
>
> *That was my reaction upon seeing Larry Levine's book,* Selling from the Heart, *featured in a LinkedIn post. What I didn't know was that I was going to receive SO MUCH more than a good business book. Let me explain.*
>
> *Larry sent a package to my home. It included the book and several additional items. There was a pair of bright red* Selling from the Heart *socks (ha!),* Selling from the Heart *concept stickers, a pen, and more. The book itself included the personal message, "Ben, always remember to sell from the heart. Be you. Larry Levine."*
>
> *This package made the best first impression of any business mailing I've ever received. As a student of helping and influencing, it was clear that Larry's approach to connecting was different and memorable.*
>
> *In the mailing, Larry never pitched anything. He simply wanted me to have his book, offered a sincere message, and delivered more value than expected. I was struck by the investment with no expectation or call to action other than to read and enjoy the book.*
>
> *What I've learned since is that Larry lives what he teaches. He was applying his Trust Formula in starting a relationship. Larry believes that Trust = Authentic Relationships (AR) + Meaningful Value (MV) x Inspirational Experiences (IE) x Disciplined Habits (DH). Rather than sending pitches for training courses, more books, or other revenue-generating items, Larry's priority was to connect, to start a relationship. His actions were authentic and delivered meaningful value. The AR + MV of the formula was amplified by the inspirational experience I had around receiving the book.*

I read Selling from the Heart. *I absolutely loved it. My role is in sales enablement. So, I shared the book with a lot of my colleagues. I reached out to Larry to thank him, and to make a personal introduction. As it turned out, nearly everyone who read the book wanted to learn more from Larry. Over the course of the year, he helped hundreds of us learn* Selling from the Heart *concepts. We formally contracted with him to support two specific sales teams in using* Selling from the Heart *and the Trust Formula ideas to produce more self-generated leads. The approach worked. We anticipate a positive bump in client retention, too.*

I've grown close to Larry and his colleagues. All of them practice the same approach—starting with the relationship and trust formula. They know us. They're not pushy. They're not pitching products or canned solutions. They listen. They help solve problems. They've worked hard to learn about our products, sales model, company, and industry. They want to know us. They're now a trusted, go-to resource. They've freely helped every individual and leader who's reached out to them. They've made a name for themselves within our company.

I'm delighted that Larry wrote Selling in a Post-Trust World: Discover the Soft Skills That Yield Hard Dollars, *which focuses exclusively on the Trust Formula. It's been a game-changer for me. I hope everyone who influences people will read this book for the benefit of their work and all their relationships.*

Thank you, Larry Levine. You and your team do noble work that helps people. Salute.

Chapter 9 Summary

1. Gratitude and passion are the two main traits of sales professionals who sell inspirational experiences.
2. You must have passion in order to inspire. If you are not passionate about what you do and how you do it, then it can be challenging to inspire others to act.
3. B2B means business to business, not boring and too bland.
4. Believe me or not, being boring is a choice. Many of you have been lulling your clients into a sense of boredom. For some, they have been doing business with you for so long that they have become numb to your services, and they have settled for boring.
5. Boring salespeople focus their attention on simply generating the next sale. On the flip side, a sales professional focuses on building long-term client relationships.

Chapter 10:

Sales Is Like a Marriage

The more you invest in a marriage,
the more valuable it becomes.
Amy Grant

I f it looks like a relationship, acts like a relationship, and smells like a relationship, then it is a relationship. The question then becomes, is it a healthy, thriving one? This is the key takeaway I want you thinking about as we explore this chapter.

In all our relationships, from family to friends to marriage, it would be accurate to say that a healthy relationship involves levels of honesty, trust, respect, fairness, love, open communication, and continual new experiences.

Relationships are a necessary part of healthy living, but there is no such thing as a perfect relationship. Relationships take time, effort, patience, respect, giving, and caring.

In healthy relationships you:

➢ Can express yourselves to one another without fear of consequences.
➢ Trust each other.

111

> ➤ Are honest with each other.
> ➤ Maintain and respect each other.
> ➤ Feel secure and comfortable.
> ➤ Appreciate each other.
> ➤ Constantly seek out new experiences.

What about your client relationships; shouldn't they consist of the same things?

If you crave a healthy business, then the relationships within that business need to be strong, vibrant, and meaningful. Would this describe the relationship with your clients?

It concerns me greatly that what constitutes a client relationship has become lost inside the sales world. Where is the significant depth and genuine meaning? Does the walk match the talk? Do you have relational congruency with your clients?

What many in sales think is a relationship may not be what it really is.

It is my belief that before anyone in sales, management, or leadership throws the terms, "We have great client relationships", "We love our clients", or "We're client-centric", on the business table, then they should give serious thought as to what they really mean. Again, does the talk match the walk?

Are You Taking Relationships for Granted?

> *Life is a precious gift—a gift we often*
> *take for granted until it is threatened.*
> **Lecrae**

Taking things for granted is an awful mistake and a huge strategic error afflicting many salespeople. Unfortunately, with sales success, often, the *complacency syndrome* kicks in. Taking your clients for granted is equivalent to shutting down your business.

You are not indispensable given the fierce competition. Your clients have options, and they will not stick around for long when complacency sets in.

According to research conducted by Microsoft and cited inside the Nextiva blog, "100 Essential Customer Service Statistics and Trends for 2022 (update: June 3rd, 2021),"

[Sixty-eight percent] of people around the world have stopped doing business with a company because of a poor customer service experience.

Let's apply this quote to salespeople, but with a twist: Could 68 percent of your clients stop doing business with you due to a poor experience or lack of attention? Just keep that in the back of your mind as we continue this chapter.

Personal Relationships, Marriage, and Sales

This is such a terrific quote courtesy of Mark Gungor, author of *Laugh Your Way to a Better Marriage*:

Marriage problems are relationship problems; they are the result of how two people interact with each other. You may abandon a troubled marriage, but you will still bring the way you interact with others along with you.

How well are you interacting with your clients? I would like for you to stop and really give some thought to the following questions:

What would happen if you went ninety days without speaking to, looking at, or even hugging your significant other? It is fair to say that most could not go more than a day. Then, why on earth do some of you go ninety days (and in most instances, even longer) without communicating and showing how much you care about your clients?

Call me delusional (I have been called worse), but let's get real. Without clients, you have no business. Without a real, loving, caring, and meaningful relationship, you have no marriage. Are you starting to smell what I am cooking?

It is time to wake up and stop taking advantage of your most precious asset—your clients!

> ## If you want a relationship, crave a relationship, and it means something to you, then you must be direct and intentional about it.

You would never say to your significant other, "It's been a bit; I'm just touching base to make sure everything is okay."

Since that's the case, then why are we calling our clients and saying the following:

- ➢ "I'm calling to see if you need anything."
- ➢ "I know it's been a bit, how are you doing."
- ➢ "My apologies for not getting with you sooner."

You can do much better. Now think about this: Are you babysitting (at best) some of your clients until someone else comes along who truly values what it means to be in a business relationship with them?

> ## Truth is in the eye of the beholder. Where do your client relationships sit in looking at this though your client's eyes? Where do the experiences you provide sit? Would you even know?

To build these types of relationships, you must understand that as humans, we crave relationships, we value them, and we desire new experiences within those relationships.

To have substantive relationships, you must have attentive and assertive conversations with your clients. This means that when you are speaking with them, you must be entirely focused on them, and learning about them with intentionality and curiosity.

Why do I say this? In a world where trust and being seen as trustworthy are at alarmingly low levels, you must prove your worth. How can you do this, though, when you rarely visit and interact with your clients?

Credibility and true meaning provide:

> ➤ Connectivity (knowing we are in this together).
> ➤ Support (knowing we are helping each other).
> ➤ Validation (knowing we feel the same way).

To build meaningful client relationships, you must continually create new memories and experiences together. This is unattainable with spotty, intermittent twice-a-year visits.

The more you give, ultimately, the more you receive. This reminds me of Winston S. Churchill who said,

We make a living by what we get. We make a life by what we give.

However, all of this begs the question: what are you giving to your clients?

A Healthy Business Relationship Is Similar to a Healthy Marriage

Just like marriages, businesses built around partnerships tend to have a better chance of success than those that aren't. When it comes to the world we live in today, I believe that business is personal.

The more personal it is, the better the connection. The more comfortable you make your clients feel about you, the more comfortable they will become in sharing their business secrets with you. This is unachievable when you rarely see your clients.

Care and inspirational experiences are how we connect. Compassion helps forge strong bonds. Letting your clients know that you will be with them every step of the way, no matter what, can go a long way in the success of any business partnership.

A past study on happy marriages conducted and published by Cornell University showed that, despite the numerous variables that exist with every relationship, there are common traits within successful marriages. These traits are as follows:

- ➢ Effective communication
- ➢ Working as a team
- ➢ Alignment of values
- ➢ Commitment

Isn't this what you desire with your client relationships?

How can you maintain happy, healthy, and harmonious relationships with your clients? You simply invest in them. You care for them. You proactively visit with them. Most of all, you continue to bring new experiences to the relationships.

What are you doing right now to ensure your client relationships don't end in a divorce?

Think of the following relationship equation with every one of your clients:

> **Meaningful Conversations x Caring x Inspirational Experiences = Trusted Relationships**

Conversations Matter

All problems exist in the absence of a good conversation.
Thomas Leonard

How good is your ability to open up, connect, and engage with other people? Now, think about your clients and answer the same question. Imagine for a moment one of your clients or a future client telling you:

- ➢ You're the first salesperson I have ever told this.
- ➢ You're the only salesperson who understands this.
- ➢ You're the first salesperson who gets me.

When you hear those words, you will know that you are on the right track.

In his book, *Don't Sweat the Small Stuff,* psychotherapist Richard Carlson writes,

> *Being listened to and heard is one of the greatest desires of the human heart.*

Think about your clients, their needs, desires, aspirations, and feelings.

Also, in his book, Carlson shares that a deep connection has four main components: listening, hearing, understanding, and validating.

> *Those who learn to listen are the most loved and respected.*
> **Richard Carlson**

When you learn to listen with intentionality, curiosity, and your heart, imagine how this will make your clients feel. How well are you making your clients feel before, during, and after doing business with them?

- ➢ What words would they use to describe how you make them feel?
- ➢ What words would they use to describe how you care about them?
- ➢ What words would they use to describe how much they trust you?

Sales Professionals Create Inspirational Moments

I want you to think back to an inspirational moment in your life. How did it make you feel? Who was the person who inspired you? Was it someone who was close to you? What did you do after you were inspired?

> **Inspiration creates a ripple. Are you creating a ripple effect within your client base, community, and the marketplace?**

Mother Teresa once said,

I alone cannot change the world, but I can cast a stone across the waters to create many ripples.

Think back to your childhood for a moment; remember skipping flat rocks across the water? Admit it, you always counted how many times it skimmed to see if you were the King or Queen of skimming rocks and have those precious bragging rights.

However, did you ever stop to notice how the water would ripple when the rock stirred it? After a moment, the ripples effortlessly flowed one into the other, creating a harmonious blending. You may have also noticed a seed pod on top of the water being gently carried by the ripples. At some point, it finds its way to the other side, and the seed it was carrying plants itself and new growth begins.

The question then becomes: what kind of ripple effect do you want to spread amongst your clients?

Without creating these inspirational ripples and moments in time with your clients, are you, in turn, growing your competitors' next great client?

The greatest gift you can give another is the purity of your attention.
Richard Moss

The attention you provide determines the experiences your clients have. Conversely, these experiences will determine the quality of your sales life.

Allow me to take you back to 1890. In his book *The Principles of Psychology, Vol.1*, William James wrote a simple statement that is packed with meaning: "My experience is what I agree to attend to."

Your attention determines the experiences you have, and the experiences you have determine the life you live. Basically, you must control your attention to control your life.

Therefore, if your experiences are based on what you agree to attend to, then the same philosophy can be applied to your clients and the experiences they have, or what they attend to, with you.

Choosing what you pay attention to, or how you divvy up your time, can be challenging, as you and I both know how busy you are running around doing "stuff."

Research continually shows us that it costs businesses significantly more to acquire new clients as opposed to retaining them. Successful businesses, leadership, and their salespeople understand the importance of providing and continually creating outstanding client relationships.

You are a huge factor in determining if your clients stay or if they go.

Allow me to take you back to the spring of 1982 and introduce you to The Clash. Their hit entitled "Should I Stay or Should I Go" further reinforces the point. I encourage you to take a listen.

Customers rely on their emotional experiences with salespeople more than any of the traditional factors, according to research by the Peppers & Rogers Group, which showed:

> ➢ 60 percent of all customers stop dealing with a company because of what they perceive as indifference on the part of salespeople.
> ➢ 70 percent of customers leave a company because of poor service, which is usually attributed to a salesperson.

What this reinforces is the importance that attitude and emotion play in determining whether your clients leave or stay. It is mission-critical for you to understand your clients' attitudes and regularly collect their feedback.

Why do your clients do business with you? Is it because they feel valued and well taken care of? I guarantee that the *why* will have a monumental impact on you and the loyalty of your clients.

As we close out this chapter, I want to share with you an unusual testimonial from my long-time friend Hugh Hornsby. He talks about my life from his perspective, and it opened my eyes to some things I had not thought about. This is an example of why you need to connect with your clients on a regular basis and get feedback from them.

> *Larry Levine has created a Sales/Leadership movement based on operating from his heart. From the conversations that I have had with Larry, he lives and executes his core values and his WHY of contributing, clarifying, and trust. His journey in sales led him through a series of unqualified managers who were put in positions of chasing the dollar without investing in people, or as he calls them empty suits!*
>
> *In his last sales job, he was kicked to the curb and forced to figure out his next steps in life—a move today he looks back on as a blessing! With the help of many of his friends, he dug deep into his heart and began a movement one small step at a time. We have talked many times about how hard it was getting started, and that many times he asked himself, WHY?*
>
> *The answer was simple: he promised himself that he would not let managers with empty suits do to others what was done to him. He was going to give people a place to go to learn a different way. He did it by surrounding himself with like-minded people—coaches, mentors, and friends—who helped him fight through the hard times.*
>
> *Understanding that salespeople are often empty suits pursuing only the sale, while not caring about the person in front of them, has set him on his way of changing mindsets. Larry has flipped the narrative, and teaches/coaches from*

an inside-out mindset. This past year, I had Larry train our team on a book read, which turned into conversations about Selling from the Heart. *During the supply chain crisis, and post-COVID-19, these conversations helped us to change the narrative with our clients. This led to the largest growth year in our company's history.*

What I admire about Larry is how humble he is, and how much he cares about helping others achieve their goals! His burning desire to continue to help people shows on his weekly podcast Selling from the Heart *with his co-host, Darrell Amy.*

In a world of management "empty suits," he is one of the people that I lean on for guidance. Larry is one of those rare people that if he says it, he lives it! He is a "say do" guy!

Reading this book, I encourage you to think about two things: sales and leadership. Most people separate the two, but both are based on the same core principles of serving and helping others getting what they want. If you are leading a team, a salesperson just getting started, an experienced sales-person wanting to learn a new way of thinking, or a manager wanting to move into leadership, I personally promise you that Larry's passion and purpose will rub off on you and your team. He left my team wanting more, and seeking knowledge to make themselves better people.

Larry has helped to begin a movement called Selling from the Heart. *This movement is not an easy one to live up to. Once you write something and then teach it daily, you must live up to what you say. As I have gotten to know Larry, I promise you that he lives up to this movement so much so that I have connected him to some of my very good friends, and he has connected me to his.*

Like-minded people tend to attract each other. If you are a like-minded person wanting to better yourself, please join the cause. We will all try to make each other better. It is time that we all embrace those that care about others and lead them by our actions not words.

On page 180 of Selling from the Heart, *Larry shares the importance of writing our manifesto: your beliefs, motives, and the intentions around each of your important topics. You are the only one that can understand what is important to you. Use that to become vulnerable by laying your cards out for everyone to see, and then start your journey of letting your heart lead you. As Larry quotes the poem* The Road Not Taken *by Robert Frost:*

Two roads diverged in a wood, and I—
I took the one less traveled by,
And that has made all the difference.
The road you decide will make all the difference.
My mentor once said, "Hugh, if you do not know where you are going, any path will take you there!" Don't let that be you!

Well done, Larry Levine! I am proud to call you my friend!

Hugh Hornsby
Vice President of Sales, Everflow Supplies

Chapter 10 Summary

1. If it looks like a relationship, acts like a relationship, and smells like a relationship, then it is a relationship. However, is it a healthy, thriving one?

2. Unfortunately for many in sales, when success sets in, the *complacency syndrome* appears. Taking your clients for granted is equivalent to shutting down your business.

3. What would happen if you went ninety days without speaking to, looking at, or even hugging your significant other? It is fair to say that most could not go more than a day. Then, why on earth do some of you go ninety days (or even longer) without communicating and showing how much you care about your clients?

4. How can you maintain happy, healthy, and harmonious relationships with your clients? You invest in them. You care for them. You proactively visit with them. Most of all, you continue to bring new experiences to the relationships. What are you doing right now to ensure your client relationships don't end in a divorce?

5. Inspiration creates a ripple. Are you creating a ripple effect within your client base, community, and the marketplace?

6. Your attention determines the experiences you have, and the experiences you have determine the life you live. Basically, you must control your attention to control your life.

Section 4:

Disciplined Habits

As we begin to round out the four facets of the Trust Formula, Disciplined Habits, the question that comes to mind is *why*? Eventually, if your why is not strong enough to hold together authentic relationships, meaningful value, and inspirational experiences, then everything starts to crumble inward.

> *Winners embrace hard work. They love the*
> *discipline of it, the trade-off they're making to win.*
> *Losers, on the other hand, see it as punishment.*
> *And that's the difference.*
> **Lou Holtz**

Are you willing to embrace hard work? Are you willing to become radically disciplined? Are you brave enough to make it happen? It is one thing to know how to change; however, it's another to be willing to do it.

This becomes the classic *can do* versus *will do* mentality. When you are not willing to change, you keep yourself in limbo or a state of complacency. You may share with others, or even yourself, how you will "try" to change. Trying is one thing, but committing to the journey is another.

When you admit that you are willing to change, you'll be surprised how the excuses soon disappear. This quote from the Bible still stands true today: "The truth shall set you free." Growing your sales will require you to do new and different things.

The question then becomes: how many of you would like to grow your sales by 50 percent? I believe I hear a resounding *yes* being shouted back to me.

Therefore,

> ➢ Are you willing to take 100 percent responsibility for making this happen?
> ➢ Are you willing to stop blaming, criticizing, and pointing fingers?
> ➢ Are you willing to get more interested in learning, rather than defending your ego?
> ➢ Are you willing to allow yourself grace as you learn and relearn new skills?

Growth and comfort do not play well together; they never have, and never will.

If you want to achieve the results that no one is achieving, then you must be willing to do the things that no one is doing.

Therefore, you must retool, reequip, and revamp parts of your processes based on a different model that calls for new approaches, new positioning, new client experiences, and new business growth. All of this should be centered on a well-organized plan.

In an ever-changing business climate, you must be willing to adapt to the rapidly evolving market conditions, digital business models, and disruptive competitors. You must become laser-focused on bringing fresh ideas and new insights in a hyper-personalized manner to your clients and future clients.

Most all, you must stop the excuses!

Champions are brilliant at the basics.
John Wooden

Far too many in sales love chasing shortcuts, automation magic, and excuses before mastering the fundamentals and becoming radically disciplined.

The legendary coaches, Vince Lombardi and John Wooden, coached, preached, and held their teams accountable to the basics. John Wooden had a trio of rules:

> *Don't whine, don't complain, and don't make excuses. Do your best. And when things go wrong, don't whine or complain or look for blame; just keep moving forward.*

The greatest skill you can master is simple: *just do the work.* Most of you don't need more time, tips, or tactical strategies. You need to do the real work with radical discipline.

Are you willing to double-down on yourself? Creating the self-discipline practices, along with inner fortitude, will ultimately lead you to sales success.

What this requires is checking your ego at the door, setting aside your fear, and turning a deaf ear to what is being said inside the sales bullpen. In fact, stop listening to all the social guru noise altogether. Amazing things will start to happen when you eliminate the unnecessary noise and excuses.

The secret to renewal and true confidence is simple:
Get back to the basics.
Tim Sanders

Stop the magical mystery sales tour that you're constantly going on. Stop letting your ego and excuses get in the way of what must be done.

How many of you will commit to developing disciplined habits to become the best that you can be? Let's find out in the following chapters.

Chapter 11:

Your Why Makes All the Difference

What is forever old is forever new.
Larry Levine

Let's ponder this statement as I take you back to the early 1900s.

The year was 1908. Napoleon Hill was a struggling magazine writer who was given the opportunity to interview Andrew Carnegie. At that time, Carnegie was the wealthiest individual in the world after selling Carnegie Steel in 1901 to J. P. Morgan (known today as J. P. Morgan Chase) for $480 million. In today's currency, this equates to well over $15 billion dollars.

Napoleon Hill met with Andrew Carnegie in the millionaire's sixty-four-room mansion in New York City. He expected the conversation to last a few minutes and then be escorted out, but to his benefit, the conversation lasted several hours.

Carnegie spent time sharing in great detail with Hill the principles and proven formula that would guide people to happiness, harmony, and prosperity. He then challenged Hill to devote the next twenty years of his life to assembling a proven formula that would propel people of all backgrounds to achieve their own success. Resoundingly, Hill accepted the challenge, which he subsequently turned into the perennial bestseller, *Think and Grow Rich.*

This entire conversation was captured in the book, *Mental Dynamite: How to Unlock the Awesome Power of You.* Early on in their conversation, Hill asked Carnegie a simple yet powerful question: "What was the driving force behind what made you so successful?" Carnegie replied, "Success for me was the combination of self-discipline and constructive habits."

Is this not a mic-drop moment? Imagine what would happen to your sales results, your client relationships, and your career if you brought self-discipline combined with constructive habits to the forefront. Layer inside of this a radical consistency plus personal accountability, and you now have the recipe for sales prosperity and longevity.

I encourage you to completely stop chasing silver bullets, hacks, tricks, and self-delusional pied pipers on social media. If you cannot do the little things correctly, then how will you ever succeed at doing the big things correctly?

You have what it takes to succeed. It starts with self-discipline, disciplined habits, personal accountability, self-worth, believability in oneself, and unwavering confidence. You can chase all the outer stuff you want, but it is not until you fix the inner stuff (*you*) that all of this starts to come to fruition.

You might be asking yourself: "Where do I start?" Allow me to share with you a few steps. Place your right hand up, your palm facing outward, look right into the mirror, and recite after me:

> ➤ I will hold myself accountable to personal growth and self-development.
> ➤ I will hold myself to the highest standards of self-discipline.
> ➤ I will hold myself radically accountable to disciplined habits.
> ➤ I will commit to leading a *Selling from the Heart* lifestyle.

Now, you are ready for the next step: unpacking your *why*.

Uncover Your Why to Uncover Your Way: Creating Self-Confidence

*If we want to feel an undying passion for our work,
if we want to feel we are contributing to something
bigger than ourselves, we all need to know our WHY.*
Simon Sinek

What is your why? To build trust, you must bring your authentic self to your clients and future clients. The question then becomes: how do you discover your authentic self?

Discovering your why is the best and simplest way to get a window into what makes you tick. We have a choice in how we show up, whether that be in sales, or in life.

Some of you will show up because of *what* you do. You will measure your success by what you sell, how well you sell it, and how many clients you secure.

Some of you will show up because of *how* you do what you do. Your success is measured in the quality, depth, and meaning of your client relationships. Lastly, some of you will show up for a definite reason. You have a cause that drives you, a belief that inspires you, and a mission that motivates you.

Find what fuels you. Live there. Grow there. Love there.
R. M. Drake

Your Why

Simon Sinek said it best, "Our goal is to surround ourselves with people who believe what we believe." Let's apply this powerful quote to your client base. Do your clients believe what you believe? Does your vision and values align to theirs? How would you know if there is such alignment?

This starts to make sense when you uncover your *why*. Your why is a statement of purpose. It describes why you do the work you do, and why you live the life you do. Your why is:

- ➤ Your calling.
- ➤ What makes you come alive.
- ➤ Your mission statement.
- ➤ A vision of your life and work.
- ➤ Your core source of motivation.

When you uncover your why, you then will be able to clearly and with confidence articulate who you are and understand why you do everything you do. When it comes to your career, uncovering your why will lead you down the right path. When it comes to your clients, sharing your why will lead to rich and more meaningful relationships.

My Why

I would be remiss if I did not share my why with you. When I uncovered and started to reflect upon it, it brought chills to my arms.

My why is as follows: I believe that success happens when I contribute to a greater cause. I want to make a difference in the lives of others. I love to support others, and relish in success that leads to the greater good.

My why was in plain sight. It's why I started the *Selling from the Heart* podcast. It's why I wrote S*elling from the Heart*, and it's why I am creating a heart-centered movement within the sales profession.

Unpacking your why creates the building block to self-confidence.

Your Why Becomes the Confidence Glue

Sales is hard and not for the weak at heart. It requires a laser-focused mindset to really be successful.

Inaction breeds doubt and fear.
Action breeds confidence and courage.
If you want to conquer fear, do not sit home
and think about it. Go out and get busy.
Dale Carnegie

One often overlooked factor to becoming a great sales professional is confidence. Therefore, the road to discovering your why is mission-critical to your career.

You must believe in yourself first. Much of what you will achieve in sales depends on how much you believe in your abilities. How many of us (me included) often lack self-belief when we need it the most?

If you do not believe in yourself, then how do you expect your clients and future clients to believe in you?

Insecurities in times of uncertainty and doubt make us believe that we are not capable of achieving our goals.

Sales professionals have the confidence to take risks that sales reps try to avoid.

Confidence Is Critical

In research conducted by Steve Martin for his book, *The Sales Strategy Playbook: The Ultimate Reference Guide to Solve Your Toughest Sales Challenges*, his goal was to understand what's really on customers' minds.

I would like to present some of the questions he focused on.

First, what are customers' perceptions of the salespeople they meet, and how do they ultimately choose between them? Only 31 percent of salespeople converse effectively with senior executives, and only 54 percent of salespeople can clearly explain how their solution positively impacts a customer's business.

This is startling and quite alarming, isn't it?

Second, how much do you believe that a lack of confidence played a significant factor with these percentages?

Third, how much do you believe that a lack of self-discipline or (conversely) a set of disciplined habits played with these percentages?

Fourth, how can your clients or future clients trust you if you do not communicate like an expert?

Please keep these questions top of mind as we make our way through the rest of this chapter.

We will focus on increasing your confidence by:

➤ Valuing yourself.
➤ Finding your passion.
➤ Changing your mindset.
➤ Uncovering your why.

Sales is about accomplishing a transfer of confidence.

Build Confidence, Value Yourself

Hands down, investing in yourself has one of the best returns on investments. A true sales professional takes responsibility in developing their gifts and talents to best serve their clients.

You must love yourself before you can expect your clients to love you.

Look in the mirror and repeat after me:

➤ I'm worth it.
➤ I'm of value.
➤ I will create the best version of me.
➤ I know my why.

Then, repeat, repeat, and repeat some more:

➤ I am a value creator.

Investing in yourself sends a powerful message not only to you, but to the business community. When you are willing to say *yes* to confidence and invest in yourself, your clients and future clients will provide you with amazing rewards.

Build Confidence, Build the Real You

Uncovering the real you is scary, but well worth the journey. You must get extremely real and radically honest with who you truly are. Rip off the mask that you are wearing. You cannot wear the mask forever. It gets tiresome and, eventually, this will destroy your authentic self.

Be the real you, not an imposter. Lord knows, there are enough empty salespeople running around the business community. Be yourself and quit trying to be someone else.

I would like to share with you a short section from *Selling from the Heart*. If you have not read it yet, I highly suggest you do. A whole section of the book is devoted to helping you become your authentic self. Simply visit https://www.sellingfromtheheart.net/book to order.

It's Time for the Real You

I have seen so many salespeople hindered from achieving success because they are trying to be someone they are not. Have you ever tracked the path of individuals who became successful and tried to mirror what they did, only to achieve lackluster results? Of course, you have.

Want to know why it did not work? Because your actions were not in line with your core self. You can be true to yourself and be successful. I am a living and breathing example of it. I have taken all that I have learned over the years, packaged it up, and made it my own. Stay true to who you are. Be genuine, be authentic—get to know yourself. Be curious and ask a ton of questions. Always ask for help. Just be the real deal—the real you!

Whenever someone would ask me, "What are you doing?" my response was always, "I'm just getting it done." Here is what I would like for you to get out of this book: stay true to who you are. Be the real deal; be genuine. Be authentic and sincere, give a rip about your career, and do what you need to do to get things done. Make things happen! Do not become *somebody you are not. Do not build a sales lie. Living a sales lie will bite you in the ass every time.*

Your Homework: Uncover Your Why and Build Your Confidence

I want to challenge you both personally and professionally in these five areas:

- ➢ Seek to become an expert
- ➢ Consistently crave feedback on you
- ➢ Become radically honest with yourself
- ➢ Create a morning ritual and rhythm
- ➢ Uncover your why

It is all about uncovering your *why* as you marry it with your *how* and *what*.

- ➢ My **WHY** is making a difference in the lives of others by supporting and contributing to their success, which leads to a greater cause.
- ➢ **HOW** I make this happen is by clarifying information so it's understandable for others. This allows them to make better decisions and move in the right direction to best suit their needs.
- ➢ **WHAT** I ultimately bring are solutions that you can trust and count on wrapped inside a trustworthy relationship.

I will ask all of you to think about the word *trust*. In a sales world sorely lacking and craving it, unpacking your *why* becomes the catalyst to consistently build upon a long-lasting and sustainable sales career.

Chapter 11 Summary

1. I encourage you to stop chasing silver bullets, hacks, tricks, and self-delusional pied pipers on social media. If you cannot do the little things correctly, then how will you ever succeed at the big things?

2. When you uncover your why, you then will be able to clearly and with confidence articulate who you are, and understand why you do everything you do. When it comes to your career, uncovering your why will lead you down the right path. When it comes to your clients, sharing your why will lead to richer and more meaningful relationships.

3. One often overlooked factor to becoming a great sales professional is confidence. Therefore, the road to discovering your why is mission-critical to your career.

4. Investing in yourself has one of the best returns on investments. A true sales professional takes responsibility in developing their gifts to best serve their clients.

5. Uncovering the real you is scary, but well worth the journey. You must get real and radically honest with who you truly are. Rip off the mask you are wearing. You cannot wear the mask forever. It gets old and, eventually, it will destroy your authentic self.

6. I want to challenge you both personally and professionally in these five areas:

   ➢ Seek to become an expert.
   ➢ Consistently crave feedback on you.
   ➢ Become radically honest with yourself.
   ➢ Create a morning ritual.
   ➢ Uncover your why.

Chapter 12:

How Are You Showing Up?

Tamara found herself gazing deeply into the mirror, not paying attention to what she saw. Her thoughts drifted back to the team meeting yesterday as the sales results from last quarter were announced. She was astonished when her name came up in the bottom five. Tamara firmly believed that she would be in the top two. As matter of fact, she had been higher in the past, and was one of the top salespeople. She was doing the same amount of work as she had done before, but her results had dropped.

Tamara knew that she was going to have make some changes next quarter or her job could be in jeopardy. She had witnessed that salespeople who were consistently at the bottom lose their jobs.

She decided to seek counsel from Sean, one of the top sales performers, when she got into the office. Sean was always friendly, engaging, and willing to help others. This conversation immediately changed the trajectory of her entire career.

"Hey Sean, do you have a minute or two to chat?" she asked.

"Sure, Tamara come on in."

As she sat down, he quicky glanced at her and said, "From the look on your face, I'm guessing you're wondering why your results were so low when they were posted yesterday?"

"Absolutely."

"I believe I can help you. Would you be open-minded to some feed-back?"

Over the next hour, they examined Tamara's work ethic. What soon became quite apparent was that her past success had bred complacency. While her efforts and results were good enough in the past, the present is the present. Tamara quickly realized that she was going to have to become more. Thus, within three months of consistent, disciplined work, she regained sitting with the top sales echelon, earning her company incentive that year.

Sales Professionals Are Radically Consistent and Disciplined

> *No, we don't control who our parents are.*
> *We don't control what color we are. We don't control*
> *what home we are born into. But we control our*
> *attitude. We control our work ethic. We control our*
> *drive and our commitment.*
> **Dabo Swinney**

You can control what you can control, and you can't control what you can't control. That being said, I believe that you are fully responsible for how you show up. Therefore, are you showing up prepared and committed to sales excellence?

If someone asked you to describe your work ethic, what would you say? Is it strong? Is it in need of some attention, or would you even know? Remember, the mirror never lies, only the person looking into it. So, tell the truth when it comes to your work ethic.

Are you cruising in the middle lane, or are you in the fast lane with your foot on the accelerator of growth?

> **Sales professionals have a strong work ethic,**
> **are radically consistent, and exude self-discipline.**
> **What about you?**

Wikipedia defines work ethic as follows:

> *It is a belief that work and diligence have a moral ben-efit and an inherent ability; it is a set of values centered on the importance of work and manifested by determination or desire to work hard.*

We live in an age of instant gratification. Thanks to LinkedIn gurus and other internet pundits, there are countless ways to success by buying their peddling wares that promise you the moon and the stars.

In sales terms, this equates to, "How fast can I succeed, or at least get to quota, with minimal amounts of work, effort, and commitment?"

Thomas Edison nailed it:

There is no substitute for hard work.

What are your daily habits, routines, and rituals? Are you committed to yourself? A strong work ethic, along with self-discipline, starts with the consistent commitment you make to yourself.

Are You Lying to Yourself?

Accomplishing your goals requires massive amounts of discipline. Words without action and discipline lead you down the path to nowhere.

Discipline means consistently doing what you tell yourself you will do without procrastination and excuses.

➢ Do you tell yourself that tomorrow, you will start prospecting, but the next day, you postpone prospecting?

➢ Do you promise yourself to read more about sales, but you fail to pick up a book?

➢ Do you promise yourself to take better care of your clients, but then find yourself looking for excuses not to do what you promised?

What this tells me is that you do not value your words, promises, or career. How can you make any real changes in your sales life, improve your sales life, or make any consistent progress if you are always lying to yourself?

Think about the following quote courtesy of the legendary Jim Rohn, and then apply these words to it: consistency, work ethic, and self-discipline.

> *You don't have to change that much for it to make a great deal of difference. A few simple disciplines can have a major impact on how your life works out in the next ninety days, let alone in the next twelve months or the next three years.*

Sales Professionals Are Consistently Consistent

> *Small disciplines repeated with consistency everyday lead to great achievements gained slowly over time.*
> **John C. Maxwell**

When it comes to sales excellence, consistency separates the good from the great.

How often have you observed someone in sales having a record year, or a series of phenomenal quarters, only to follow it up with spates of mediocrity and below-average performance?

Consistency differentiates the successful from the unsuccessful, and sales professionals from sales reps. Radical consistency will change the course of your sales life forever! Give some thought to how Dictionary.com defines consistency:

> *Steadfast adherence to the same principles, course, form, etc.*

Therefore,

- ➤ Consistency allows you to measure results.
- ➤ Consistency yields accountability.
- ➤ Consistency builds upon your reputation.

Unfortunately, many salespeople today are consistently inconsistent.

Consistency Starts by Doing Your Job

To be consistent is to completely dedicate yourself to a task, activity, or goal. It means to fully remain engaged without distractions and excuses. I am amazed at how many in sales negotiate with themselves the non-negotiable aspects of their job.

Consistency requires commitment and massive amounts of self-discipline. It requires you to commit yourself to a sustained effort of action over the long-term. Keep your word to yourself and your family that you will follow through with what you set out to do.

Do your job! This is what you signed up for when you decided to work within the sales profession. Did anyone twist your arm to get into sales, or did you choose it?

> **What happened to self-discipline, working hard, self-accountability, practice, preparation, a commitment to excellence, and a no-excuse mindset?**

Bill Belichick, head coach of the New England Patriots, said it best,

Ignore the noise and do your job.

The Mental Struggle

Short-term thinking combined with instant gratification squashes any aspects of consistency. I am concerned that when many in sales fail to gain immediate results from their actions, they play mental gymnastics as to why they should continue those actions. Case in point: prospecting. That's why my favorite quote from *Selling from the Heart* rings true:

*Salespeople have hypnotized themselves into
believing what they are not doing, doesn't work.*

Why do many in sales find it difficult to remain consistent? Call it lack of focus, vision, purpose, or passion, many simply lack commitment and discipline to stick with something short-term for long-term gain.

Stop the excuses and get to work. There are no quick results and no silver bullet moments when it comes to a commitment to consistency.

Consistency is all about small incremental improvements over time. The results you are after will eventually come; however, they will come over an extended period of time when you commit to consistently doing the right things.

> *Success is nothing more than a few simple disciplines practiced every day.*
> **Jim Rohn**

To remain consistent, you must commit to being consistent. Sales professionals realize that the greatest power lies in the present moment. They understand that consistency demands attentiveness, presence, and a positive mindset. It demands they remain disciplined to the moment without exception, and no questions asked.

> *What comes into our mind, comes out in our life.*
> **Craig Groeschel**

They consistently apply themselves over an extended time period to reap long-term sales rewards. Success is not a light switch that you turn on and off.

Create a Plan

Creating consistency requires planning.

A sales professional is forward-thinking as they plan, prepare, and practice consistent behaviors. They understand their core activities are built around their values, purpose, plan, and goals.

If for any reason their priorities are not in alignment with these areas, they acknowledge it and realign to it. Are you connecting with your core values, your personal mission, and the quiet voice in your head?

As you look in the mirror, ask yourself these questions:

> ➤ What is my mission statement?
> ➤ What are my values?
> ➤ What am I grateful for?

When you can answer those questions, you can then start to create a daily plan centered on who you truly are, which makes it easier to accomplish because you are not fighting yourself.

Massive Action

The path to success is to take massive, determined action.
Tony Robbins

Consistency (along with focus) comes in the form of proper preparation, planning, and practice. A professional prepares each day with consistent action. They mentally prepare themselves with daily doses of self-reflection.

They ask of themselves:

> ➤ What actions do I need to do to achieve my goals?
> ➤ What actions do I need to repeat to achieve my goals?

Sales professionals are laser-focused. They have a clear idea of what needs to happen to achieve their desired outcomes. What are your desired outcomes?

They understand what consistent repetitive activities they must do, and then they take massive action. What are you doing right now to take massive action?

It's All About Consistency

Your sales life is too precious to waste. Your future rests solely in your hands.

> ➤ You alone decide what your fate will be.
> ➤ You alone choose to be distracted.

➢ You alone can only decide to take action.
➢ You alone must hold yourself accountable. The hardest part of being self-disciplined is doing it every day.

You may not see immediate results, but over time and with consistent action you will build the foundations of a meaningful sales life. In a sales world where trust and credibility are anemically low, think about the following:

➢ Consistency in your character develops integrity.
➢ Consistency in your attitude creates trust.
➢ Consistency in your self-leadership builds influence.

Consistency and Discipline: The Missing Links to Sales Success

Disciplined habits are like a fine red wine; they age with time and tender loving care. Are you starting to gain an appreciation of disciplined habits? This becomes an asset yielding you monumental dividends. To reinforce the importance of these assets, let's dive into some finance 101.

Appreciating assets are those that increase in value over time. Think of disciplined habits in the same manner. Appreciation can be caused by numerous factors. Let's focus in on these two:

➢ An increase in demand for your asset.
➢ A decrease in supply of your asset.

Could bringing disciplined habits and self-discipline to your sales career cause *you* as the asset to appreciate in value? I submit to you that the answer is yes!

How much it appreciates is usually tied to risk. When the risk is low (like with certificates of deposit or bonds), the asset's value does not go up significantly. However, with higher risks, the potential payoffs can also be greater.

How much risk are you willing to take on to grow yourself?

Conversely, a depreciating asset is one that goes down in value over time. A car is a prime example, as vehicles are infamous for plummeting in value the instant they are driven off the lot. Unless your car is a classic, you will not get what you paid for it when it is time to sell it.

A lack of disciplined habits becomes your depreciating asset. Are your clients getting what they paid for with you?

As we close out the chapter, I would like to remind you to check out the free resources section at www.sellinginaposttrustworld.com. There, you will find material that will allow you to explore the topic more fully.

Chapter 12 Summary

1. You can control what you can control, and you can't control what you can't control. That being said, you are fully responsible for how you show up. Are you showing up prepared and committed to sales excellence?

2. We live in an age of *instant gratification*, and thanks to LinkedIn gurus and other online pundits, there are countless ways to success by buying their peddling wares that promise you everything without any effort.

3. To be consistent is to completely dedicate yourself to a task or goal. It means to completely remain engaged without distractions and excuses. Today, many in sales negotiate with themselves the non-negotiable aspects of their job!

4. Short-term thinking combined with instant gratification squashes any aspects of consistency. I am concerned that when many in sales fail to gain immediate results from their actions, they play mental gymnastics as to why they should continue those actions.

5. A sales professional is forward-thinking as they plan, prepare, and practice consistent behaviors. They understand that their core activities are built on their values, purpose, plan, and goals.

6. Sales professionals are laser-focused. They have a clear idea of what needs to happen to achieve their desired outcomes. What are your desired outcomes? They understand what consistent repetitive activities they must do, and then they take massive action. What are you doing right now to take massive action?

7. Disciplined habits are like a fine red wine; they age with time and tender loving care. Are you starting to gain an appreciation of disciplined habits? This becomes an asset yielding you monumental dividends.

Chapter 13:

The Two Greatest Assets to Your Sales Growth

Self-discipline; the real 'secret' to success. If ever there were a true magical ingredient to achieve success, self-discipline would be it.
Andrew Carnegie

Self-discipline is the difference between the sales dreamer and the sales doer. Self-growth is what makes self-discipline possible. Many salespeople talk a good story about what they are going to do. Some even put their intentions into practice. However, few salespeople can stick to their plans.

Without self-discipline in following through, there can be no improvement. The depth and breadth of your discipline will determine the longevity of your improvement.

I am confident that many of you want to grow your sales, gain more new clients, and become your very best; that is why you are reading this book.

However,

Are you willing to invest in yourself to be the best?

➢ Are you a dedicated life-long sales learner?
➢ Are you taking what you are learning and creating better sales habits?

> **True sales professionals are constantly growing. They devote the time needed to improve themselves and their sales craft. Do you?**

High-achieving sales professionals push themselves further, harder, and stronger than anyone else ever will.

The great Walt Disney once said,

> *Whatever you do, do it well. Do it so well that when people see you do it, they will want to come back and see you do it again, and they will want to bring others and show them how well you do what you do.*

Think about this quote. Now, apply it to your sales career, and then to how you are working with your clients. Does this quote apply to you, or do you need to do some work on it?

> **If you want to substantially grow your sales, you must be willing to dig in deep.**

You must commit to knowing and growing yourself.

Self-Growth Becomes the Accelerator to Sales Growth

At this very moment in time, if you were asked what your strengths are, would you be able to provide an immediate answer with confidence and clarity?

If you stumble and bumble needing paragraphs to explain, you may not clearly know your strengths. If you struggle to explain what you do best in a few concise sentences, then quite possibly, you have not devoted the time to become conscious of your strengths.

Greek philosopher Thales of Miletus, renowned as one of the legendary Seven Wise Men, once said,

If you don't take the time to clearly know yourself, you won't be able to raise your influential value.

Therefore, if you want to exponentially grow your sales, then raise your influential value. You raise your influential value by getting to know the real you. Are you willing to embark on the journey?

When you're able to be honest with yourself about who you are and finally can present your authentic true self to the world, you feel so much better about yourself, and it makes it easier for everyone else to feel better about you.
Gus Kenworthy

What you may be hiding from the business world and your clients could be preventing you from monumental growth.

Please pause for a moment to deeply reflect upon these questions:

➢ Are you living as the real you, and not someone else?
➢ Do your thoughts match your actions?
➢ Does your walk match your talk?
➢ Are you spotlighting your positive aspects?

I believe that when you are constantly living a lie, it rises to the surface sooner or later. Living a sales lie as somebody you are not is even worse. All this does is ultimately screw with your career and sales results.

Are you tracking with me so far? How are you holding up?

Your greatest accomplishment is combining self-discipline with self-growth—this is the one-two punch needed to skyrocket your sales career.

What Are You Building?

In the poem written by Charles C. Finn, "Please Hear What I am Not Saying," the opening lines read,

> *Don't be fooled by me. Don't be fooled by the face*
> *I wear, for I wear a mask, a thousand masks, masks*
> *that I am afraid to take off and none of them is me.*

High-achieving professionals are not self-centered. The best of the best incorporate self-reflection and are truly aware of who they are. They hold themselves accountable, and with discipline they strive to become better every single day. They love eating humble pie for breakfast, and look forward to a day full of learning as they serve their clients.

We have all heard the age-old saying, "People do business with people they know, like, and trust." Therefore, what are you doing to double-down on your people and relational skills? How do you become more recognizable inside your client base? How do you build your authority within your client base? Are you becoming the subject matter expert within your client base?

If you want to exponentially grow your sales, you must bring the real version of yourself to the business table! You must become disciplined, and commit to self-growth.

Will You Commit?

No personal sales success, achievement, or goal can be realized without self-discipline. Think about the following quote:

People who lack self-discipline are often the victims of those who do have self-discipline.
Robert Kiyosaki

To become the master of your own destiny, you must commit to self-discipline and self-growth. Focus on the long-term benefits instead of the short-term discomfort. The inner work you do on yourself fuels the outer success you will have in sales.

Self-Discipline Without Excuses: Driving Monumental Sales Growth

Ultimately, you have complete control and command over the success you have in sales.

Self-discipline is as old as mankind. The Stoics were big on the three disciplines of desire, action, and assent.

> ➢ Desire has to do with acceptance of our fate.
> ➢ Action has to do with the love of mankind.
> ➢ Assent has to do with mindfulness of our judgments.

Think about the Stoics and reflect on the following questions:

> ➢ Where is your desire to succeed, or have you accepted your sales fate?
> ➢ Where is your love for mankind—your clients?
> ➢ Are you being mindful and not casting judgment, especially with your clients?

Even the Buddhist monks treated discipline as the holy grail. As the Dali Lama once said,

A disciplined mind leads to happiness, and an undisciplined mind leads to suffering.

There is no free ride to your sales success. There is no easy button to press. There are no quick tactics, tips, or tricks, though many of you will try to find them.

Without disciplined work, dedication, and an extreme tolerance for frustration and setbacks, you will struggle to become a sales champion.

Stop the sales suffering! A disciplined mind is a terrible thing to waste.

> **Self-discipline is your core personal power.**
> **It is the source of all other powers.**

To quote, *David Eagleman*, the author of *Incognito: The Secret Lives of the Brain*,

> *Our behavior is simply the result of the many battles between short-term and long-term desires in our brain. If that is the case, then self-discipline is your ability to choose the part of you that should win the battles that matter.*
>
> *Exercise this power within your brain, and you strengthen it. You will have gained the fulfillment of knowing you're doing your best. Do this day after day, week over week, and month over month, expressing the best there is in you, and you will live with the calmness of having no regrets.*

Improve Self-Discipline, Adopt No Excuses

One of my favorite quotes is by Craig Groeschel:

> *We can make excuses, or we can make progress,*
> *but we can't make both.*

When you combine self-discipline with a no-excuses attitude, it creates sales success. When you hold yourself personally accountable, you will graduate from a sales rep to a sales professional.

Sales professionals:

➢ Have a no-excuse mentality.
➢ Don't point fingers when they fail to hit their sales plan.
➢ Simply do the things that sales reps find excuses not to do.
➢ Hold themselves accountable even if their manager doesn't.

Excuses stunt both sales and relational growth. They are invented reasons we create to defend our behavior, postpone taking action, or simply neglecting responsibility.

Excuses are mainly a means of placing the blame of an internal problem on an external condition.

Excuses are tools of incompetence used to build bridges to nowhere and monuments of nothingness, and those who use them seldom specialize in anything else.
Vernon Brundage Jr.

There are numerous reasons why salespeople make excuses, including the following:

➢ Fear of failure.
➢ Fear of success.
➢ Fear of change.
➢ Fear of uncertainty.
➢ Fear of what others may have to say.

Did you notice the word they all began with? Fear. This is the one word you need to get rid of if you want self-discipline in your life. You cannot be afraid of what others may think. You need to be concerned with taking smart, decisive action and let the rest fall to the wayside.

The roadmap to your success is based upon disciplined work, personal ownership, and practice. It takes self-discipline combined with a no-excuses thought process to achieve monumental sales success.

You need to acquire the habit of work and demonstrate personal initiative to get ahead in life. There is no benefit to procrastinating or performing mediocre work. Ideas are the beginning points of all fortunes, but it takes action to keep them alive.
Napoleon Hill

Back in 1908, in that infamous conversation between Napoleon Hill and Andrew Carnegie, Hill went on to say, "I deduce that self-discipline is largely a matter of constructive habits. Is that the idea?"

Carnegie replied, "What a person is and what a person accomplishes both in failure and success is the result of that person's habits. Gaining control of these habits goes a long way toward the attainment of self-discipline."

This conversation took place well over 100 years ago and is still fully applicable today. The question now becomes: what will you do about it and when will you start?

Self-Discipline Requires a Special Mindset

Sales professionals are business athletes. What separates elite salespeople from the rest? I believe that elite salespeople have a "next level" mindset. They constantly challenge themselves. Are you doing the same?

Elite salespeople push themselves to practice. They pay attention to the little things on a consistent basis and continually focus on positive work habits. Can this be said about you?

Could you become more consistent in sales if you changed your mindset?

What would happen to your sales results with an improvement in your preparation, practice, and how you mentally prepared for sales day?

Stop Living a Sales Lie: Develop Discipline

Unfortunately, most sales reps would rather get by with subpar work ethics, coupled with minimal levels of practice, while entertaining themselves on social media. Then, they wonder why their results continually have them in the sales management dog house.

These sales reps do not want to put in the extra effort to become more focused or self-disciplined. The secret to success is mental. The secret to success is in your hands and your actions, not in your mouth.

The secret to success is quite simple to understand, yet so difficult to consistently put into action.

Do you have what it takes to take your career to the next level? Can you honestly put your actions where your mouth is? Are you willing to walk the talk?

Dr. Napoleon Hill said it the best,

> *Self-discipline begins with the mastery of your thoughts. If you don't control what you think, you can't control what you do. Simply, self-discipline enables you to think first and act afterward.*

The possession of self-discipline (without excuses) enables you to choose, and then persevere with actions, thoughts, and behaviors. This all leads to improvement and sales success.

In the next chapter, we will tie this all together. With encouragement, and before you turn the page, please set aside the time to examine yourself and your sales results, and become radically honest with yourself. This will help you immensely as you design your action plan going forward and into the next chapter.

Chapter 13 Summary

1. True sales professionals are constantly growing. They devote the time needed to improve themselves and their sales craft.

2. Deeply reflect upon these questions:

   ➢ Are you living as the real you, and not someone else?
   ➢ Do your thoughts match your actions?
   ➢ Does your walk match your talk?
   ➢ Are you spotlighting your positive aspects?

3. High-achieving professionals are not self-centered. The best of the best incorporate self-reflection and are truly aware of who they are. They hold themselves accountable, and with discipline, they strive to become better every single day. They love eating humble pie for breakfast, and look forward to a day full of learning as they serve their clients.

4. There is no free ride to your sales success. There is no easy button to press. There are no quick tactics, tips, or tricks. Without disciplined work, dedication, and an extreme tolerance for frustration and setbacks, you will struggle to become a sales champion.

5. Sales professionals:

   ➢ Have a no-excuse mentality.
   ➢ Don't point fingers when they fail to hit their sales plan.
   ➢ Simply do the things that sales reps find excuses not to do.
   ➢ Hold themselves accountable even if their manager doesn't.

7. Many sales reps often do not want to put in the extra effort to become more focused or self-disciplined. The secret to success is mental. The secret to success is in your hands and your actions, not in your mouth. The secret to success is quite simple to understand, yet so difficult to consistently put into action.

Chapter 14:

The Journey Continues

Life is like a bicycle; you won't fall off unless you stop pedaling. It's all about balance. Challenge your limits, but always remember life is not a race, but a journey.
Based on quotes by Albert Einstein and Claude Pepper

t is so unreal, as we find our time together coming to an end. When I set out on the voyage to write *Selling from the Heart*, I could barely envision writing one book, let alone writing a second.

I am a firm believer that things happen for a reason (such as reading this book). Life is one monumental journey. The highs are high, and the lows are low. It's a rollercoaster of emotions, just as it is in sales.

From time to time, it seems impossible: the rollercoaster never ends, and your goals, dreams, and aspirations will never be reached. At other times, you find your heart soaring as you reach a new level in your personal life and professional career. In both instances, I imagine a majority of the success you achieved was because you looked deep inside yourself and changed the things that needed to be changed.

I want to let you know that I am proud of you. You have made it this far and have not quit. You have removed the temptations and the excuses. You have made the decision to become a trusted sales professional. You have committed to do the hard work. You decided to peek inside yourself to become the real authentic you. You are dedicated to taking a hard stance and saying no to being that pushy, desperate, and untrustworthy sales rep. You care about yourself, your clients, and making a difference. I applaud you for it. You are taking the road not travelled, and you will thus reap mammoth-sized results.

As we bring our time together to a close, my gift to you is a game plan to implement, so you will be able to continue in your career with confidence. This all starts with taking a step back to look at what we learned during our time together.

The Trust Formula

(AR + MV) x IE x DH = TR

The key drivers are Authentic Relationship (AR) plus Meaningful Value (MV). The multipliers are Inspirational Experiences (IE) fueled by Disciplined Habits (DH). This, my friends, equals Trusted Relationships.

Trust is the foundation of all relationships; without it, relationships crumble.

Tragically, though, the mindset within the sales community has been one of "all about me", as opposed to "all about us". It has been about "How fast can I get to quota with the least amount of work?". Charm, charisma, and sales pizazz does not work any longer, especially in this post-trust world.

I am concerned, and you should be as well, that trust is anemically low in our society. However, you can do something about it. You control how you show up, how you interact with others, and how you carry yourself. I believe that when you show up as being trustworthy, you will stand out against all others. Still, trust must be earned, and it starts with your first interaction.

Not much will happen unless you put it into action. This applies to how you build trust. This is where the trust formula comes in. Take massive action on it!

Each piece of the formula layers upon the other. If everything is not aligned, the results will be nil. (Think back to your school days and what happens when you multiple something by zero!)

Authentic Relationships

Remember the reference to the "Man in the Mirror" song as we embarked on our journey together? How are your mirror moments of reflection working for you? Are you still holding back from making the changes needed to transform yourself, your career, and your sales results? Do not be afraid to ask yourself tough questions. When answered, growth happens. Becoming your authentic self is magical. Watch what starts to happen next.

The transformation process begins by casting aside the four killers of authenticity: excuses, fear, ego, and emotional baggage. Each one of them creates blockages in your life. This not only hinders you from being your true self, but also creates the emptiness, steering your sales career in a vastly different direction.

During this transformation of becoming your true self, your internal light starts to shine bright as you become a B.E.A.C.O.N. of hope to others.

B: Belief
E: Encouragement
A: Attitude
C: Compassion
O: Offer to help
N: Nourish

When you care about your clients, they immediately take notice. What soon develops is safety based upon trust. This means letting your internal secret sauce and special gifts shine brightly, allowing you to stand out as a sales professional, as opposed to a sales rep. You are now placing people, your clients, over profits.

The more you invest in your clients, the more they will invest in you. Remember, you are developing a client community and networks of people who know, like, and trust you. This will ultimately build your relational wealth, and propel your sales to new heights.

Meaningful Value

Authentic relationships and meaningful value are two sides of the trust coin. They must be used in tandem if you desire trusted client relationships. The glue holding all of this together are real conversations rich with intentionality, curiosity, and heart.

How do you have these conversations? It's quite simple: you stop acting like a salesperson. Allow yourself to become vulnerable. Engage in proactive, genuine, and unscripted conversations. Initially, this might be uncomfortable, but relational growth occurs through healthy and assertive conversations.

What do proactive conversations look like?

➢ You prevent problems before they arise.
➢ You answer questions before they ask you.
➢ You have open conversations about difficult things.
➢ They are planned, purposeful, and deliver on their promises.
➢ They are about the client (not you).

If you are going to engage in valuable conversations, then you must become valuable and indispensable to your clients. You must become an educator of ideas. You do this by becoming a student of your clients' business. You must develop deep business knowledge and conversational skills.

In today's radically competitive world, forward-thinking salespeople consistently earn the right to sit at the table. They do this by having . . .

A keenness and depth of perception, discernment, or discrimination especially in practical matters. A power to see what is not evident to the average mind.
Merriam-Webster Dictionary definition of "acumen"

No longer do salespeople have a knowledge advantage. With that in mind, how are you standing out amongst the sales masses? I believe that you rise to the top through strategic help, creating real value, and a willingness to do the things no other salesperson is doing.

To deliver meaningful value with conviction, you must mature into a sales professional who is curious, caring, and collaborative. You should become extremely inquisitive, allowing the conversation to go where it will, even if this has absolutely nothing to do with selling anything.

To connect with the heart, you must:

➢ Make yourself available to serve.
➢ Pay attention to your clients.
➢ Complete every task with equal dedication.
➢ Become faithful and trustworthy.
➢ Care about your career, your clients, and their livelihood.

Inspirational Experiences

How good are you at inspiring others? The ability to inspire is one key leadership skill distinguishing great leaders from average ones. Such leaders have a clear vision, mission, and commitment to integrity. This fuels them in everything they do to make the world a better place.

I wholeheartedly believe that these characteristics can be applied to a *Selling from the Heart* professional. Sales professionals are indeed leaders. They inspire their clients into business betterment through heart-felt experiences.

Inspiration combined with memorable experiences become the catalysts for deep client loyalty and long-term sustainable relationships. The consummate professional helps their clients paint a picture of what could be, as together they cast a vision and work towards a brighter future.

One aspect of inspiring your clients is how you make them feel. Do they feel valued and appreciated? One sure-fire way to do so is by creating those moments, memories, and experiences they will never forget.

Here comes the mirror moment. With honesty answer the following:

➢ Do I really understand what my clients want?
➢ Am I relevant in their eyes?
➢ How am I making them feel when I see, speak, or interact with them?

A failure to create memorable experiences grows the competition's next great client!

I have seen this scenario play out repeatedly. A sales rep who creates bored clients will soon see their clients find a sales professional who delivers a great experience. You can no longer rest on the laurels of yesteryear. A comfortable sales mindset—believing your clients will never leave you—is a dangerous game to play.

Remember, sales is like a marriage. It involves building, maintaining, and nurturing long-term relationships. Are you ignoring yours? In healthy relationships, you can express yourselves to one another without fear of consequences. You trust and respect each other. You are honest, secure, and comfortable together.

Disciplined Habits

The foundational glue to the trust formula is disciplined habits. Radical discipline is being able to do on a regular basis what others will not. One bedrock of disciplined habits is knowing your purpose.

Are you disciplined enough to do the things that others in sales are unwilling to do?

Once you establish your purpose, you can then take ownership for how you show up. Are you consistent in how you show up, or are you chasing shiny objects in search of the holy sales grail?

Sales professionals have one remarkable work ethic: they do not lie to themselves. The promises made are fulfilled with the utmost of integrity. They understand that being consistent is hard work. They recognize the mental component, and they embrace it.

I highly recommend reading *The Power to Change: Mastering the Habits That Matter Most* by Craig Groeschel.

He opens part three of the book by asking,

Assuming today was a normal day, what did you do? Whatever you did, chances are it was pretty much what you did yesterday and what you will do tomorrow.

Follow along with me as I share this excerpt from his book. As you read this, please think of your sales life.

Much of what we do is not the result of conscious choices, but daily habits. Duke University did a study and found that 40 percent of actions people take in any given day are the result not of decisions, but of habits. We do much of what we do because it's what we always do. Your choices create the course and contours of your life. Your decisions determine your destiny.

If you want to change your sales life, change your sales habits. If you want to change the direction of your sales life, change your sales habits. If you want to become a sales professional, remove the excuses. When you combine all four elements of the trust formula, unshakeable trust is created.

I want to share a testimonial with you from Brad Rennick that demonstrates the power of *Selling from the Heart*.

Although it only feels like yesterday, it was May 4, 2020 when Larry Levine entered my network and, more importantly, my heart. I remember our first encounter well. Of course, it was virtual as we were all trying to navigate through our newly imposed social restrictions. It was a time when we were all looking for a human connection in a purely digital environment.

I was watching a video conversation where Larry was participating. He talked about the inner component of being okay with yourself. It resonated with me as I was not only on my own personal and professional journey, I was also leading a sales team through an unprecedented selling environment and an organizational restructuring. I knew then that I needed more.

In a sales world where most trainers drove technique and tactics as the foundation for sales development, Larry was unique in that he talked about relationships, empathy, and connecting on a personal level. I liked the video, and immediately Larry reached out with an invite, which I accepted without hesitation. It was a few weeks before we could connect virtually, and when we did, the Selling from the Heart *journey began.*

Larry spent a lot of time getting to understand me, our business, the team, and our company's expectations. Through the many sessions and insightful questions, Larry was always in teaching mode, wanting only to assist our leaders to inspire and coach a very diverse technical selling team. We quickly embraced everything that embodied Selling from the Heart. *Larry's blogs, podcasts, LinkedIn posts, and book became our go-to source for developing authenticity, trust, relationships, and empathy.*

We needed to develop our technical sales reps into relationship professionals. Larry supported our team in the transformation by participating in our virtual sales meetings, our weekly update sessions, and being present in our employee-inspired book club that was initiated with Selling from the Heart. *Larry went above and beyond, as he offered many of our team individual coaching sessions. Plus, he helped to develop sales professionals while helping our team and organization to fundamentally change our culture.*

The Sales Leadership Team began measuring our relationship funnel and quickly determined that as our relationships flourished, so did our opportunities. Our daily vocabulary evolved to include terms like authenticity, sales professional, self-reflection, servant mindset, and empathy while truly understanding that we were no longer empty suits.

This book and his movement have become the foundation for our teams. Selling from the Heart *is part of our recruiting process as we work diligently to differentiate between sales professionals and empty suits.* Selling from the Heart *isn't an option; it's a lifestyle and an expectation for all of our sales professionals to embrace. As a wise man once declared, "Authenticity is a choice."*

Larry Levine is the real thing; he is down to earth, caring, understanding, trustworthy, and authentic. He is everything that he coaches. Larry has taught us to invest in ourselves, be accountable, be authentic, and always self-reflect. Thank you for bringing humanity and humility back to our industry. Above all, thank you for reaching out and becoming part of my life and my inspiration for ongoing growth and development. We can't wait to continue the journey!

Brad Rennick
Vice President of Global Sales, Dwyer Omega

The Next Steps: Will You Lead a Trust-Based Lifestyle?

In a world that is starving, craving, and yearning for trust, what will you do about it? Moving forward, what will you be willing to do to change the perception of sales?

Reflect upon Psalm 15:2 (NASB) with me:

"He who walks with integrity, and works righteousness, And speaks truth in his heart."

Will you be willing to hold yourself accountable in speaking the truth and leading a *Selling from the Heart* lifestyle?

Honesty and truthfulness are two key ingredients of personal integrity. The righteous person is not only honest with others (their clients and future clients), but also with and about themselves, as well. What is your truth?

In building your truth to becoming someone worth trusting, I have to ask you, what is your vision? What propels you?

I love what Craig Groeschel has to say about vision:

Without vision, people become comfortable with the status quo. Later, they grow to love the status quo. Eventually, they'll give their best to protect what is, never dreaming about what could or should be.

How will you conquer the status quo? How will you avoid being labeled empty?

Your Vision Will Propel You

If you want the people you serve (your clients) to embrace you, then you must be clear about who you are, what you do, why it matters, and where you're headed.

➢ What impact would you like to have with your clients?
➢ What impact would you like to have within the marketplace?
➢ What impact would you like to have within your community?

What's your endgame in sales? Is it to make a sale, collect a check, or to make a difference? You must deliver tangible results with purpose and meaning, not sales rhetoric. Creating your sales purpose not only transforms sales effectiveness, but it also provides insulation from the price hammer. Leaders cast vision; they are visionaries. They're purposeful, they have a plan, and they lead from the heart.

Nobody exemplified this more than Walt Disney. As it says in Chapter 3 of *Lead Like Walt* by Pat Williams,

*Leadership requires that we communicate our vision in
a powerful, persuasive, memorable way.*

Walt Disney turned his visions into reality through the power of communication. Are you communicating your purpose, your vision, and your plan?

Your Sales Life Is Too Short

You deserve a career where you have a sense of purpose and a vision that guides you. Sales professionals do not leave such factors up to their company or their management team. It is up to you to define what you do with your sales career. Thus,

➢ Know what motivates you.
➢ Find a mentor or a business coach.
➢ Self-reflect and crave self-improvement.

When you have purpose, vision and disciplined habits create clarity. Clarity creates freedom. It removes the roadblocks, even the mental ones. To bring all of this to fruition, you must gain a simple understanding of what you want and how you will reach your destiny. Clarity becomes high-octane fuel to vision and purpose. If you are not clear about your *why* and *how*, then you will never lift your vision off the ground.

Clarity brings:

➤ A sense of direction.
➤ A sense of meaning.
➤ A sense of passion.
➤ A sense of personal freedom.

Do you believe what you do matters? If so, then it is up to you to make it happen. *Selling from the Heart* starts with caring about yourself. With trust and credibility being at anemically low levels, your journey to trustworthiness starts with the trust you build with yourself.

Are you ready to start your journey to building trust? The decision is all yours.

I will leave you all with a portion of a poem by Catherine Pulsipher, "People Know":

Always be that person who is trusting
Then life will need no adjusting.
People know what you say and do
Are a reflection of the true you.

This why I believe your clients and future clients would rather connect and do business with a sales professional who sells from the heart as opposed to a sales rep who is an empty suit.

Now It Is Up to You

In a post-trust world, you have a choice to make. You can remain being labeled a sales rep struggling to consistently hit quota, always wondering if the next time they let someone go, this might just be you.

Or, you can transform into the sales professional you are meant to be: the person standing out head and shoulders above the rest, and someone who firmly believes they are a trusted partner, not an empty sales rep.

What will you choose? I must admit that being a sales professional is hard work. You are going to have to do things you may not want to at first, but as you develop, you will reap what you sow.

In closing, I encourage you to enroll in the Trust Formula Mini-Course at www.sellinginaposttrustworld.com. This course will help you to implement what you have learned here. Plus, you will get additional resources throughout the year to help you in your sales journey. If you love podcasts, then check out the *Selling from the Heart Podcast*. Each week, my co-host Darrell Amy and I interview the top people in the sales industry who will share with you what it means to sell from the heart and how to do it authentically.

My hope for you is this: that you become a sales professional who not only reaches all of your goals, but helps your clients reach theirs, too.

I am forever grateful to you for going on this journey with me.

The best is yet to come.

Larry Levine

About Larry Levine

Larry Levine is the international best-selling author of *Selling from the Heart: How Your Authentic Self Sells You,* and the co-host of the *Selling from the Heart* podcast. Blending a heart of service with over three decades of in-the-field sales experience, Larry helps sales professionals develop a mindset and skill set for authentic success. In a post-trust sales world, Larry helps sales teams leverage the power of authenticity to  grow revenue, grow themselves, and enhance the lives of their clients.

Larry has coached sales professionals across the world, from tenured reps to new millennials entering the salesforce. They all appreciate the practical, real, raw, relevant, relatable, and "street-savvy" nature of his coaching.

Larry believes people would rather do business with a sales professional who sells from the heart as opposed to a sales rep who is an empty suit.

A free ebook edition is available with the purchase of this book.

To claim your free ebook edition:

1. Visit MorganJamesBOGO.com
2. Sign your name CLEARLY in the space
3. Complete the form and submit a photo of the entire copyright page
4. You or your friend can download the ebook to your preferred device

Morgan James BOGO™

A **FREE** ebook edition is available for you or a friend with the purchase of this print book.

CLEARLY SIGN YOUR NAME ABOVE

Instructions to claim your free ebook edition:
1. Visit MorganJamesBOGO.com
2. Sign your name CLEARLY in the space above
3. Complete the form and submit a photo of this entire page
4. You or your friend can download the ebook to your preferred device

Print & Digital Together Forever.

Snap a photo

Free ebook

Read anywhere

Printed in the USA
CPSIA information can be obtained
at www.ICGtesting.com
CBHW031523010324
4721CB00004B/17